D0559379

TEN SKILLS OF HIGHLY EFFECTIVE PRINCIPALS

HOW TO ORDER THIS BOOK

BY PHONE: 800-233-9936 or 717-291-5609, 8AM–5PM Eastern Time

BY FAX: 717-295-4538

BY MAIL: Order Department
Technomic Publishing Company, Inc.
851 New Holland Avenue, Box 3535
Lancaster, PA 17604, U.S.A.

BY CREDIT CARD: American Express, VISA, MasterCard

BY WWW SITE: http://www.techpub.com

PERMISSION TO PHOTOCOPY–POLICY STATEMENT

Authorization to photocopy items for internal or personal use, or the internal or personal use of spe-
cific clients, is granted by Technomic Publishing Co., Inc. provided that the base fee of US $3.00 per
copy, plus US $ .25 per page is paid directly to Copyright Clearance Center, 222 Rosewood Drive,
Danvers, MA 01923, USA. For those organizations that have been granted a photocopy license by
CCC, a separate system of payment has been arranged. The fee code for users of the Transactional
Reporting Service is 1-56676/96 $5.00 + $ .25.

TEN
SKILLS
OF
HIGHLY
EFFECTIVE
PRINCIPALS

June H. Schmieder, Ph.D.
Associate Professor, Pepperdine University
Donald Cairns, Ed.D.
Associate Professor, Montana State University

TECHNOMIC
PUBLISHING CO., INC.
LANCASTER · BASEL

Ten Skills of Highly Effective Principals
a **TECHNOMIC** ᵍpublication

Published in the Western Hemisphere by
Technomic Publishing Company, Inc.
851 New Holland Avenue, Box 3535
Lancaster, Pennsylvania 17604 U.S.A.

Distributed in the Rest of the World by
Technomic Publishing AG
Missionsstrasse 44
CH-4055 Basel, Switzerland

Printed in the United States of America
10 9 8 7 6 5 4 3 2 1

Main entry under title:
   Ten Skills of Highly Effective Principals

A Technomic Publishing Company book
Bibliography: p. 99

Library of Congress Catalog Card No. 95-62235
ISBN No. 1-56676-381-9

CONTENTS

THE thoughts for this book began to form from an article that I developed because of an interest in the education of school principals. I had served in the public schools for over twenty years and had recognized the importance of the school principal as the key figure in the school. The study focused on the novice principal. In addition, I surveyed over 650 principals and superintendents in California to determine the skills and habits they thought were necessary to be a successful school principal.

Don Cairns of Montana State was also interested in the work, as similar discussions were going on among his faculty. He brought in the prospective of the rural school district superintendent, which is crucial to understanding the issue.

Finally, Carol McGrevin and I worked for the past three years on a project at Pepperdine University to train principals so that they would be prepared for the rigors of this tough job. We wanted to include an extensive fieldwork component as well as reflective thinking about the decisions they would make and the leadership activities they were assuming.

Gratitude is given to the following for their thoughts and support during this time: Doctors David Bowick, Terry Cannings, Nancy Magnusson Fagan, Cara Garcia, Woody Hughes, Tom Ikeda, Robert Paull, Sid Stokes and Arthur Townley. They have provided the support, encouragement, and ideas for a rigorous and intellectually rewarding principal-preparation program at Pepperdine University called the Pepperdine University Educational Leadership Academy.

A host of articles and books proclaim the importance of the school principal—a position that assumes more importance as we move into deeper levels of decentralized decision making. The principal is a curriculum coordinator, crisis facilitator, therapist, advocate for oppressed children, bus stop monitor, temporary custodian and maker of difficult decisions—all within one position and all within our day. If one were to observe both a successful principal and an unsuccessful principal, it might be a difficult task to identify the exact skills and traits that distinguish one from the other. In fact, the successful principal might be having a "bad day," and the observer will end up mystified as to the reasons why this principal has the reputation of being successful. Although both may be using skills related to overall success, only one may be successful.

SKILLS

What skills are required for success and survival? Is there a list of specific skills essential to survival? What is a skill? Even though specific skills might be elusive, they are in the repertoire of the successful principal. If a principal is observed over a length of time, the skills clearly emerge. Every superintendent can identify his or her "best and brightest" principals and is quick to point out those who are not. Acknowledging the belief that effective administration is part wizardry and part learned skill, certain competencies or mind-sets could serve as a blueprint for the novice principal, or even the experienced principal. Is it possible to learn these skills? In most cases, yes. However, the first step is to become aware of the fact that they exist, and that you, as a beginning principal, need to add them to your repertoire.

It may be useful to define a "skill." A skill is a proficiency, ability, or dexterity that usually requires learning or training to master. This text is helpful to beginning and experienced principals because it defines those skills that educators perceive as most likely to foster success. The text may be used to supplement others that focus on educational administrative concepts.

Many studies conclude that by the end of the first year, the "writing is on the wall" as to the ultimate success or failure of the principal. Therefore, learning on the job is a precarious plan at best and one that should be pursued cautiously. An interesting study on principalship by Parkay, Currie, and Rhodes (1992) developed a five-stage path for the beginning principal that involves survival, control, stability, educational leadership, and professional actualization. Principals enter this continuum at different points. Furthermore, it is the authors' contention that the quicker the novice moves through that sensitive and harrowing first level of survival and attains control, the more secure he or she will be.

With this in mind, we have created a series of case studies that have their roots in actual occurrences. No matter how difficult that first year is, we recognize that no principal works in a vacuum and that the smart administrator will call on colleagues (sometimes in the next school district) for advice. We do not advocate the case study as a panacea for all learning. It is assumed that two or more individuals might work on each case study and develop a group solution. It is important for each participant to complete the Lincoln/Machiavelli decision instrument so that a map of the individual's decision-making pattern can be developed at the end of the text.

WHY SELECT THE CASE STUDY APPROACH?

Case studies have been used for over 125 years in professional programs as a method for incorporating practical issues into an academic program. Even though law schools have used the case study approach for years, this method has not been used extensively in educational administration programs. (The case study method, in fact, brought both the Harvard Law School and the Harvard Business School into national prominence.) Most case studies are far more complex than a simple text illustrates. They involve decision making that forces administrators to think in terms of breaking the case study into simpler frameworks.

The case studies in this text will provide the reader the opportunity to identify the primary problem, any secondary problems, and discuss alternative solutions.

WHY THESE PARTICULAR CASE STUDIES?

Since this text is based upon a series of case studies, it is important to recognize the critical skills necessary for principal success and to incorporate lessons learned from these studies into actual behavior. A study of 450 California principals and 206 California superintendents asked the administrators to identify the most critical skills needed by a beginning principal. Of 1,125 principals who had been appointed to their position in 1989 or later, 450 usable questionnaires were returned yielding a 40% return rate. Of the 435 superintendents surveyed, 208 were returned yielding a 57% return rate.

The principals in the study completed a forty-five-item questionnaire that asked for background data related to gender, age, and years in education, as well as an assessment of university-based certification. The questionnaire also asked respondents to assess the importance of twenty-four skills normally associated with the role of the principal on a five-point Likert scale. The items on the scale were derived from the work of Daresh and Playko (1989), which involved the use of the Delphi technique to determine the nature of specific skills sought and valued by superintendents as they selected new principals for their school districts. The first eight items related to skills that traditionally are considered ''technical'' or ''how-to'' skills. The second set of eight items related to self-awareness skills.

The superintendent questionnaire was similar to the principal questionnaire. The survey also included an item eliciting the superintendents' beliefs on the biggest challenges for beginning principals, as well as the superintendents' perception of how well-prepared aspiring principals were to meet these challenges. The third part of the questionnaire included the twenty-four critical skill items described in the principal questionnaire.

The results listed in Table 1 indicate strong agreement among and between principals and superintendents regarding critical skills that are needed for new principals. The top ten skills are indicated in boldface.

Table 1. Mean Scores and Ranking of Critical Skills Survey Items by Superintendents and Principals.

Numerical Skills	Type of Skill	Principal Mean	Ranks/ Ranking	Superinten- dent Mean	Ranks/ Ranking
1. Knowing how to evaluate staff (e.g., procedures for the task, and also substance: What do standards really mean?).	Technical	4.51	3	4.56	3
2. Knowing how to facilitate/conduct group meetings (large and small).	Technical	4.34	6	4.29	6
3. Knowing how to design and implement a data-based improvement process, including goal-setting and evaluating.	Technical	3.94	12	3.81	14
4. Knowing how to develop and monitor a budget.	Technical	3.96	11	3.82	13
5. Knowing how to organize and conduct parent-teacher-student conferences.	Technical	3.90	13	3.87	11
6. Knowing how to establish a scheduling program for students and staff (master schedule).	Technical	3.72	21	3.49	21
7. Awareness of the state code and other issues associated with school law.	Technical	3.82	16	3.41	22
8. Knowing how to manage food service, custodial and secretarial staff.	Technical	3.48	23	3.13	24
9. Establishing a positive and cooperative relationship with other administrators in the district.	Socialization	3.76	20	3.76	16
10. Knowing how to delineate employee roles in a school setting.	Technical	3.81	17	3.84	12
11. Knowing how to relate to school board members and central office personnel.	Socialization	3.83	15	3.69	19
12. Knowing where the ethical limits exist within the district or building and balancing that knowledge with one's own professional values.	Self-awareness	4.04	10	4.12	9
13. Understanding how the principalship changes one's family and other personal relationships.	Self-awareness	3.80	18	3.61	20

Table 1. (continued).

Numerical Skills	Type of Skill	Principal Mean	Ranks/Ranking	Superinten-dent Mean	Ranks/Ranking
14. Developing interpersonal networking skills that may be used with individuals inside and outside the school system.	Socialization	3.90	14	3.80	15
15. Knowing how to encourage involvement by all parties in the educational community.	Socialization	4.16	9	4.20	8
16. Knowing how to develop positive relationships with other organizations and agencies located in the school's surrounding community.	Socialization	3.79	19	3.74	17
17. Demonstrating an awareness of what it means to possess organizational power and authority.	Self-awareness	3.69	22	3.71	18
18. Demonstrating an awareness of why one was selected for a leadership position in the first place.	Self-awareness	3.39	24	3.40	23
19. Portraying a sense of self-confidence on the job.	Self-awareness	4.27	7	4.22	7
20. Having a vision along with an understanding of the steps needed to achieve relevant goals.	Self-awareness	4.69	1	4.70	1
21. Demonstrating a desire to make a significant difference in the lives of staff and students.	Self-awareness	4.61	2	4.60	2
22. Being aware of one's biases, strengths and weaknesses.	Self-awareness	4.41	5	4.33	5
23. Understanding that change is ongoing, and that it results in a continually changing vision of the principalship.	Self-awareness	4.44	4	4.39	4
24. Knowing how to assess job responsibilities in terms of the "real role" of the principalship.	Self-awareness	4.22	8	4.05	10

TOP TEN CRITICAL SKILLS

As a result of surveying 450 school principals in California, a list of the top ten critical skills necessary for principalship success was developed. Included here are the top ten skills as well as a description of what each skill entails.

The top ten skills include:

(*1*) Having a vision along with an understanding of the steps needed to achieve relevant goals.

(*2*) Demonstrating a desire to make a significant difference in the lives of staff and students.

(*3*) Knowing how to evaluate staff (e.g., procedures for the task and also substance: What do standards really mean?)

(*4*) Understanding that change is ongoing and that it results in a continually changing vision of the principalship.

(*5*) Being aware of one's biases, strengths, and weaknesses.

(*6*) Knowing how to facilitate/conduct group meetings (large and small).

(*7*) Portraying a sense of self-confidence on the job.

(*8*) Knowing how to assess job responsibilities in terms of the "real role" of the principalship.

(*9*) Knowing how to encourage involvement by all parties in the educational community.

(*10*) Knowing where the ethical limits exist within the district or building and balancing that knowledge with one's own professional values.

1. *Having a Vision along with an Understanding of the Steps Needed to Achieve Relevant Goals*

Each principal must have a vision for his or her school that has been developed outside of the community and staff. This vision should be compatible with the vision for the district that has been developed by the superintendent and board. The principal also needs to outline the steps required to achieve this vision for the school. Without these steps, or intermediate goals, the vision will be meaningless.

2. Demonstrating a Desire to Make a Significant Difference in the Lives of Staff and Students

Many surveys have asked education professionals why they are interested in the field. The answer received most often is the desire of these professionals to make a significant difference in the lives of students. This skill relates to the overall set of abilities in the self-awareness category.

3. Knowing How to Evaluate Staff (e.g., Procedures for the Task and Also Substance: What Do Standards Really Mean?)

Knowing how to evaluate others is a skill that takes a long time to acquire. Good evaluators have the ability to maintain motivation and still point out areas that need improvement. Most principals are required to evaluate their teachers at least once per year. The beginning principal who masters this skill early ensures that substance is part of his or her evaluation process.

4. Understanding That Change Is Ongoing and That It Results in a Continually Changing Vision of the Principalship

Unless they are familiar with the dynamics of change, principals will not survive long. Curriculum changes, personnel changes, and standards change. Working with staff in an ocean of change is one of the prime skills of a principal.

5. Being Aware of One's Biases, Strengths, and Weaknesses

Seven out of the top ten critical skills involve self-awareness. Principals should be aware of their strengths and weaknesses. In this way, they can hire people who complement them with strengths they do not possess.

6. Knowing How to Facilitate/Conduct Group Meetings (Large and Small)

Much of the time of the principal is taken up with meetings—both large and small. Meetings are the way much of the work in education is accomplished—from curriculum revision to building positive community relationships. Dozens of skills help to make even a simple meeting successful. Principals are judged on the success of their meetings, so the ability to conduct meetings is a skill worth cultivating.

7. *Portraying a Sense of Self-Confidence on the Job*

Principals feel that they must portray a strong sense of self and mission on the job and provide a strong sense of direction for the teacher team at the school. The principal must exhibit a strong sense of self-confidence in dealing with students, staff, and community.

8. *Knowing How to Assess Job Responsibilities in Terms of the "Real Role" of the Principalship*

With the increasing importance of decentralization, the principal should continually assess the real responsibilities of the job. Job responsibility for a principal may range from acting as a custodian to acting as a psychotherapist. Many of the tasks of the principal are related to motivating, evaluating, setting a standard for instructional leadership, and leading a team of educators on a powerful mission.

9. *Knowing How to Encourage Involvement by All Parties in the Educational Community*

One of the major tasks of the school principal is to implement strategies that will encourage involvement of all parties at the school site. Strategies used by the school principal involve many sophisticated public-relations skills.

10. *Knowing Where the Ethical Limits Exist within the District or Building and Balancing That Knowledge with One's Own Professional Values*

Of the twenty-four skills that were rated by principals as being important to the novice principal, knowing ethical limits emerged as the tenth most important skill. Knowing the ethical boundaries of all jobs assumed a very high priority in the ratings.

When asked to evaluate their training, both novice and experienced principals felt that there should be more emphasis on practical information, case studies, and internships. Most state certification programs for the principalship are now emphasizing more practical experiences than they did previously. This change sets the stage for this text.

The ten skills of highly successful principals are included in the sixteen case studies that follow. Each case study illustrates at least one of the key skills that it is important for novice and experienced principals to possess.

WHY SELECT THESE PARTICULAR SIXTEEN STUDIES?

A set of case studies can address issues in a way that a textbook or even an internship cannot. The sixteen studies include issues related to teacher incompetence, substance abuse by employees, book censorship, budget reductions, demands of community-based special interest groups, and interpersonal relationships. The studies have been selected for the following reasons:

(*1*) Each incident actually occurred during the tenure of a school principal on the job for less than two years. Each case study caused an agonizing time for the novice principal and in some cases affected the individual's position or entire career.

(*2*) Each case study is representative of a "critical incident." The survival of the novice principal depends on the successful resolution of critical incidents.

(*3*) The sixteen studies are related to the skills rated as the most necessary to surviving the first years of the principalship.

There are several enhancements to the typical case study text including:

(*1*) The opinions of both Lincoln and Machiavelli are presented at the end of each case study. Even though these are judgmental, the opinions are based upon the actual written opinions of the two leaders.

(*2*) Discussion questions are intended to stimulate conversation about the case study.

(*3*) Suggested readings guide the reader to pursue a deeper understanding of the issues and to link theory and practice. Theory and
practice go hand in hand.

(*4*) The reader is asked to mark on a Lincoln/Machiavelli Decision
Continuum where his or her final decision would fall. These
decisions are marked on a master chart in the Appendix to determine
if there is a pattern in the type of decisions the reader is making.

WHY INCLUDE THE OPINIONS OF THE LINCOLN AND MACHIAVELLI SCHOLARS?

Lincoln and Machiavelli were masters of their time. Each used his
intelligence to acquire skills to analyze and overcome critical incidents.
Lincoln, of course, addressed the most potentially destructive event in
our history—the Civil War. Machiavelli addressed the political quag-
mires in Italy, providing advice to an Italian prince who was trying
desperately to retain his power.

Lincoln was a great administrator who spent a vast amount of time
talking with his troops. He preferred fireside chats in the muddy bat-
tlefields and frigid tents to addressing politicians in the cold halls of
Washington. Lincoln could speak to Congress effectively and then carry
on a conversation with a soldier using homilies that drove his point home.
His Gettysburg Address contained many classic themes, but has been
analyzed as written at the tenth-grade level. Lincoln could change his
spoken and written word to match the level of his audience, and his
respect for the individual shows through in all his communications.

Machiavelli was a canny Italian nobleman who was writing advice for
his beloved prince. The warring factions and principalities fighting
during this time can be compared to the political nature of a school
district. Some administrators find that their decisions may fall anywhere
on the spectrum depending on the case under discussion. In any group
of advisers there are those who fall all along the continuum from the
laissez-faire to authoritarian approach. Any principal should be aware
of his or her decision-making style.

To paraphrase Machiavelli: It is the wise school principal who knows
his or her decision-making style and knows where his or her feelings lie
in relation to his or her advisers. This is how princes stay in control of
their principalities.

NOTE TO INSTRUCTORS REGARDING HOW TO UTILIZE THIS TEXT

The text should be used to supplement other principal-preparation texts. Authors that you might read include Hersey and Blanchard (leadership theory), Hall and Hord (change theory), English (curricular issues), Hoy and Miskel (organizational behavior issues), and Alexander and Alexander (legal issues).

The book is of value to the instructor because it involves discussing cases with students and helping them to solve hypothetical issues.

It is of additional value to students because it informs them of the skills that principals perceive as the most critical to their success.

Matrix for Identifying Primary Levels of Position, School Level and Location.

Case Number:	1	2	3	4	5	6	7	8	9	10	11	12	13	14	15	16
Administrative Position																
Superintendent									X			X				
Asst. superintendent							X			X	X		X	X		X
High school principal		X	X	X	X							X			X	
Middle school principal						X										
Elementary school principal	X						X									
Assistant principal						X										
Other central office								X								
Level of School																
School district							X	X	X							
High school		X	X	X	X					X	X		X	X		
Middle school																X
Elementary school	X					X	X		X			X			X	
Location																
Rural	X									X						
Suburban		X				X	X						X			X
Urban/large city											X					
Town/small city														X	X	
Suburban/rural			X	X	X				X			X				

Top 24 Skills and Chapters and Where They Are Found.

Critical Skills	Chapter(s)
1. Knowing how to evaluate staff	1, 2, 12, 13, 15
2. Knowing how to facilitate group meetings	5, 6, 7, 8, 9, 14, 15, 16
3. Knowing how to design a data-based improvement process	7, 12, 15
4. Knowing how to develop and monitor a budget	7
5. Knowing how to conduct parent-teacher-student conferences	8,15
6. Knowing how to establish a scheduling system	7
7. Awareness of the state code	1, 2, 3, 4, 11, 12
8. Knowing how to manage operational services	7, 8, 13
9. Establishing a positive relationship with other administrators	6, 13, 16
10. Knowing how to delineate employee roles	1, 5, 15, 16
11. Knowing how to relate to school board members	6, 8, 12
12. Knowing where the ethical limits exist	1, 2, 3, 4
13. Understanding how the principalship changes one's family relationships	10,13
14. Developing interpersonal networking skills	3, 5, 9, 14, 15, 16
15. Knowing how to encourage involvement by all parties	3, 5, 6, 9, 14, 16
16. Maintaining positive relationships with other agencies	9,15
17. Knowing organizational power and authority	1,6
18. Knowing why one was selected for leadership	13
19. Portraying self-confidence on the job	1, 9, 12, 13, 14
20. Having a vision along with knowledge of how to achieve it	3, 12, 15, 16
21. Desiring to make a difference in the lives of staff and students	1, 3, 4, 5, 13
22. Aware of one's biases, strengths and weaknesses	9
23. Understanding that change is ongoing	3, 13, 14
24. Knowing how to assess job responsibilities	3, 13

CHAPTER 1

Teacher Competence

OF all of the skills needed by the successful building-level administrator, the ability to engage the teaching staff in a meaningful evaluative process is a critical skill. However, as research has revealed (Cairns, 1989), very few principals are perceived as being capable of generating true instructional improvement. The reasons are many and may be attributed to deficiency of supervisory skills on the part of the building level administrator, miscommunications, failure to take adequate time to complete the task at hand, insecurities on the part of the teacher and the principal, and other issues. All of these arguments make instructional improvement strategies difficult to initiate and complete successfully.

This exercise is designed to give the beginning administrator a sense of the complexity one encounters when attempting an intervention with a troubled teacher. The building-level administrator learns very soon that all aspects of the school culture begin to weave together. Law, leadership, instructional theory, politics, and the building-level culture braid together to create problems that may be difficult to solve. Yet they must be managed in such a way that the problem does not reoccur, children are not damaged, lives are affected positively, and the instructional culture of the school improves.

While a seemingly monumental chore, the task must be undertaken. The new administrator's hand will not be held during the process, and the sense of isolation will become overwhelming at times. However, if schools are to improve at the instructional level, this process must be undertaken on a regular basis. The situation below is designed to give a sense of what is involved in the complex world of ''instructional improvement.''

Relevant Skills

1. Knowing how to evaluate staff
7. Awareness of the state code
10. Knowing how to delineate employee roles
12. Knowing where the ethical limits exist
17. Knowing organizational power and authority
19. Portraying self-confidence on the job
21. Desiring to make a difference in the lives of staff and students

---

MR. COULSON DRAINS THE SWAMP

The Tidewater School is an administrative unit of a larger school system offering a larger variety of programs and is a community in transition. Tidewater has traditionally been associated with a logging economy, though this is changing as resources dwindle. The school attendance area is composed of the following three groups: 1) young professionals represented by business owners, bankers, attorneys, and upper income couples; 2) working class parents who support themselves by logging or working for the paper pulp mill and wood products-related services; and 3) people residing in substandard housing close to the Big Muddy River who could best be described as working poor. An important, though small group of people residing in the Big Muddy River School District is retired and has little contact with the school. Tidewater School could be described as suburban/rural in composition. Community service is dominated by the upper crust of Tidewater society in the form of an international service group, while the Volunteer Fire Department is composed of blue collar workers from the wood products industry. There are no other service clubs in the community.

The local five-member board of directors is composed of experienced board members who could best be described as a mix of professional, working-class, and wood products-related members. Recently split votes have begun to occur. The gender composition reflects one woman and four men. The lone female board member "seeks out" teachers in order to verify whether "morale" is positive or not. The superintendent is likeable enough, but is known as "upwardly mobile" with a pragmatic outlook on school administration. At times, Mr. Coulson, the principal, has observed the superintendent arrive at decisions and recommendations based on pure politics instead of on a concern for the education program.

Mr. Coulson had barely settled into the principal's chair of Tidewater School when he received a call from Mr. Dave Benson, a former school principal from Tidewater. "How's it going with old 17?" Dave asked. Not knowing who "old 17" was, Mr. Coulson asked, "Who's 'old 17'"? "You'll find out," replied Dave, changing the subject. Later Mr. Coulson found out that "old 17" was the first-grade teacher in room 17.

Mr. Coulson found that "old 17" had been employed for twelve years by Tidewater and, therefore, is tenured. Evaluations from past principals do not reflect anything negative about her or her teaching skills. Yet rumors persist about Mrs. Bridges. While people are not shy about approaching Mr. Coulson about Mrs. Bridges and her perceived lack of teaching skills, all complaints are of a very general nature. Most complaints originate from the working class and low-income people in the district, with the upper-income people expressing strong support for Mrs. Bridges.

Upon investigation, Mr. Coulson found the following facts:

(*1*) Mrs. Bridges was the former consort of a former principal still living and working within the district. The principal still maintained a high profile in a local service club.

(*2*) Mrs. Bridges and her husband are close friends with the former principal and his wife.

(*3*) The wife of the former principal is related to the Tidewater Schools reading teacher, who is the sister of the mayor of Tidewater.

(*4*) Mrs. Bridges is very active in the Tidewater Education Association and the Parent-Teacher Association.

(*5*) Mrs. Bridges is not pleasant to work with professionally owing to her openly hostile attitude toward the administration. Her attitude conveys the message (sometimes openly) that all administrators are nothing more than highly incompetent, self-serving demagogues.

As far as could be established by Mr. Coulson, Mrs. Bridges has a tendency to verbally berate children from low-income families, gossip about staff members and school children, and has different standards of behavior for children from upper-income and low-income brackets. Mr. Coulson has observed that Mrs. Bridges does not plan consistently, is late for work, and deviates from the school- and district-defined curriculum.

Prior to Thanksgiving break, Mrs. Smith requested an audience with Mr. Coulson about Justin Smith (a first-grade boy). It seems that Justin forgot his library books, and Mrs. Bridges severely reprimanded him in front of the other first-grade children for over thirty minutes. Additionally, Justin has had to be treated for head lice and often comes to school unkempt. Mrs. Smith alleges that the combination of the two issues has caused Mrs. Bridges to take a dislike to her and her children. When confronted, Mrs. Bridges denies that she ever berated any child or was personally offended by any child with head lice.

Mr. Coulson is unsure what to do. The superintendent says it's Mr. Coulson's call, but he is not so sure the support he desires is there. Feeling uneasy he retreats to his office to ponder his alternatives.

What would you do? Would you take your lessons from Machiavelli or from Abraham Lincoln?

Machiavelli

Develop alliances, as the fortunes of the leader are entirely dependent upon the goodwill of the resident barons. These relationships are unstable and volatile. Stable relationships like living plants in nature require strong roots, and strong roots take time to develop. However, time is short, and the potential for much harm is present. Use Mrs. Smith to spread discontent and rumor by allegedly filing a discrimination lawsuit against Mrs. Bridges. Ingratiate yourself to the PTA in order to form alliances within the school and community. Have the school nurse speak on matters of health (lice), invite a professor of education to speak to the PTA about good classroom management and how to spot discrimination, seek out an attorney to speak to the PTA and the Lions Club about the legal issues of schools' allowing discrimination to continue, and send your school board to training workshops sponsored by the legal profession on school law. Keep a working record of all the misdeeds of Mrs. Bridges for future reference. Scheme to place the responsibility of inaction on the board and superintendent. Remember—the true measure of a good leader is the ability to create and sustain a highly functional organization.

Lincoln

Build strong alliances on personal and professional levels. Learn how people will respond. Maintain your own sense of integrity and ethics. Communicate your beliefs and values to others; trust in the people and the people will trust in you. Communicate your message in terms of what the common person is able to understand (homilies). A wise leader only fights one fight at a time. Send Mrs. Bridges to staff development workshops on health issues, classroom management, and discipline. Try to understand what causes her behavior in order to find the correct solution. Use nonrenewal or dismissal only as the final and last resort. Act only out of necessity and not out of vengeance or spite. Be sincere in your desire to assist those with difficult problems.

DISCUSSION QUESTIONS

(*1*) In what way would the complex social structure of the Tidewater School District complicate any action planned?

(*2*) Are the flaws in Mrs. Bridges's behavior and teaching serious enough to warrant action? What action should be contemplated? Are those actions defensible from a legal and moral point of view?

(*3*) What are the pros and cons of the different strategies as outlined by Machiavelli and Abraham Lincoln? How might they be similar and how might they differ?

(*4*) Compare the two strategies proposed in the case study with your own leadership style.

(*5*) Is there a difference between a general lack of teaching skills and other inappropriate teacher behaviors?

(*6*) Do rural schools have different value systems than what would be found in larger more urban-suburban areas?

(*7*) Would a simple transfer of Mrs. Bridges be a possible viable solution? Would it be more viable in a larger school system as compared to a smaller school system?

(*8*) Do the behaviors exhibited by Mrs. Bridges meet your state's "good cause standard" for dismissal or nonrenewal? What would need to be proven in order to meet a "good cause standard"?

(*9*) Compare the two leadership recommendations of Lincoln and Machiavelli. Are there any similarities to their approaches?

SUGGESTED READINGS

Acheson, K. and Gall, M. (1992). *Techniques in the clinical supervision of teacher: Preservice and inservice applications.* White Plains, NY: Longman Publishing Co.

Alexander, K. and Alexander, D. (1992). *American public school law.* Third edition. St. Paul, MN: West Publishing Co.

Cairns, Donald V. (1990). Differences in organizational structure between selected rural elementary and secondary schools in Washington state. Unpublished doctoral dissertation, Washington State University, Pullman.

Hall, G. and Hord, S. (1987). *Change in schools: Facilitating the process.* Albany, NY: State University of New York Press.

Hersey, P. and Blanchard, K. (1988). *Management of organizational behavior: Utilizing human resources.* Fifth edition. Englewood Cliffs, NJ: Prentice Hall.

Kerr, N. (1964). The school board as an agency of legitimation. *Sociology of Education,* 38:34–59.

Kirkendall, R. (1966). Discriminating social, economic, and political characteristics of hanging versus stable policy making systems in school districts. Unpublished doctoral dissertation, Claremont Graduate School.

Orlich, D. (1989). *Staff development: Enhancing the human potential.* Boston, MA: Allyn & Bacon Publishing.

Vidich, A. and Bensman, J. (1968). *Small town in mass society: Class, power, and religion in a rural community.* Princeton, NJ: Princeton University Press.

CHAPTER 2

Personnel/Substance Abuse

IN school administration it seems that nothing comes easy. Problems that confront the school administrator will eventually span the entire range of human behavior, provided that one stays in the field of school administration long enough. One key to surviving and thriving in the position of school administration is the ability to master critical skills.

Attending to personnel matters that lie outside of the teacher/staff position description is a very important part of the building-level administrator's job. It is not easy to do the right thing at the right time for the most seasoned of school administrators. The set of decisions made by a building-level administrator may consequently determine the success of personnel sanctions when litigated in the courts. Dealing with persons with problems is difficult enough, even when the interplay of school politics is absent. Frequently, but not always, the personnel issues that challenge the school administrator have been dormant for some time. It is not uncommon in schools of all sizes to encounter personnel matters that have been handed down from one building administrator to another like "hand-me-down clothes."

THE DIPSOMANIACAL COUNSELOR

Rick Smith, the principal of Eastside High School, had been on the job for only two months when a delegation of parents came to visit him. As he listened to the parents and took notes, he became dismayed at the problem placed before him.

The delegation consisted of the wife of the minister of the local Southern Baptist church, the wife of the mayor, and one other prominent parent from the community. While the group was not overwhelming in numbers, the community power structure appeared well-represented.

Relevant Skills

1. Knowing how to evaluate staff
7. Awareness of the state code
12. Knowing where the ethical limits exist

"We have come to you requesting that something be done about Mr. Caring, the school counselor. He is drunk in his office when he visits with students about their programs, career choices, and other school related issues," related the minister's wife. "We want to put a stop to his wicked drunkenness. We have a God-fearing school here and we want to keep it that way."

"Yes," chimed in another parent, "if the school can't reflect the values of the community, then we will have no choice but to remove our children and school them at home. It may be that for all we know, he is a drug addict and a boozer."

Rick paused before responding. "Well," he stated, "I will investigate your allegations, but you must remember that he is a tenured teacher. As such, he is entitled to more than a cursory hearing or investigation."

"God's commandments are what we follow in our lives, not the artificial courts of mortals," the minister's wife stated. "Either you go after him or we go after you!"

After they had left the school, Rick pulled Mr. Caring's file. In the personnel file were only those items that pertained to the initial date of hire, records of courses taken, sick leave used and accumulated, and other normal personnel information. There were no records of disciplinary sanctions, and all evaluations related to his position were above average. His record of absenteeism was slightly higher than average, but not excessive. Rick found not one item referencing an alcohol abuse problem. From his personal experience, he had noticed that Caring did not attend some faculty meetings and slept during others. The only reference that he found to any problem came from a small bit of information from the school secretary. "Mr. Caring sure does use a lot of Listerine," she stated.

Later, during the weekend, as he pondered the problem that had been set before him, he decided to take a walk. Head down and deep in thought he proceeded down the sidewalk. When he first looked up, it was as if his feet had taken him to the direct source of his vexation. Standing in front of the high school building, Rick entered and went directly to the counselor's office.

Rick Smith placed his hand upon the counselor's desk. "What hidden secrets are in the desk? What do I do if I find evidence of substance abuse on the job?" he asked himself.

Without further thought he opened the drawers of the desk. Tucked away he found a small, brown shoe box. It was clearly labeled, "Property of Mr. Caring." Inside the box he found the following items: a large bottle of mouthwash, a small bottle of Four Roses, and a small package of fine, white powder.

What would you do if you were Mr. Smith? Would you follow the advice from Machiavelli or from Lincoln?

Machiavelli

Nothing is as difficult as retaining power in mixed principalities— especially the baronies under your command. Your position is due to the power and influence of the baronies and so it is unwise to cause them harm. A leader should attempt to keep the goodwill of the people and help maintain the loyalty of their barons. However, a strong leader cannot be close friends with the barons, the people, nor the soldiers.

Consider investigating the desk. Claim that you were checking on which desks needed to be replaced when the box accidentally fell out. If there is evidence, use it; if not, then investigate further. In any case, the counselor must go, but with cause, so as to hold you blameless.

Lincoln

In all matters keep your honor. Do not open the desk and investigate. Remember that General Grant was also an alcoholic. He was also instrumental in saving the Union, and for that he is much revered. The only way to deal with this illness is to be open. If I knew what brand of whiskey General Grant drank, I would have bought him a case, because the man fought so well.

Confront the counselor with the allegations gently and tactfully. Provide him with treatment if necessary. Your understanding will improve your standing with the locals at all levels.

STUDY QUESTIONS

(*1*) What does the law in your state have to say about people with alcohol- or drug-related problems? Does your state have a process to hear complaints about teachers, administrators, and others holding a certificate? If so, how does it work or not work? Could it be strengthened?

(*2*) Does the Americans with Disabilities Act apply here? If so, what are the legal obligations of the district to Mr. Caring?

(*3*) Does probable cause enter this investigation? If so, what would be the possible ruling on any evidence of alcohol or drugs found in the shoe box at a hearing? Would probable cause impact the possible outcome of a disciplinary hearing?

(*4*) Are moral issues at stake for both the district and Mr. Caring?

(*5*) How might the politics of the district impact a school board's ability to deal with the issues in this case?

(*6*) What about Mr. Caring's right to a private life? When might the right to privacy be abrogated by the right of the state to protect children?

(*7*) Investigate the rate of success of persons involved in ''kicking'' a drug or alcohol problem? How might that affect your decisions?

(*8*) How might your leadership style or value system affect what you would do? What do you think of Mr. Smith opening the shoe box labeled ''Property of Mr. Caring''?

(*9*) How might the teaching staff react to the moral issues? Would your building support the principal or the counselor?

(*10*) What would be the position of the teachers' union? Do law and ethics (morality) sometimes make strange bedfellows? Provide examples where something legal may be immoral or not correct?

(*11*) Is it possible to do the correct thing and yet harm the district? Would the reverse be true?

SUGGESTED READINGS

Black, J. and English, F. (1986). *What they don't tell you in schools of education about school administration.* Lancaster, PA: Technomic Publishing Co., Inc., pp. 53–62.

Bonnie, P. T. (1994). *Federal Disability Law, American Disabilities Act.* West Nutshell Series. St. Paul, MN: West Publishing Co.

Heslep, R. (1988). *Professional ethics and the Georgia public school administrator.* Athens, GA: University of Georgia, Bureau of Educational Services.

Lyman, L. (1988). The principal: Responsive leadership in times of change. Paper presented at the Annual Meeting of United School Administrators of Kansas. Wichita, KS (ERIC Document Reproduction Services No. ED 293 201).

National Center of Alcohol Education. (1982). *Planning alcoholism counseling education (PACE): A curriculum and instructional resource guide.* Arlington, VA: National Center for Alcohol Education.

Roberts, W. (1987). *Leadership Secrets of Attila the Hun.* New York, NY: Warner Books.

Valente, William D. (1994). *Law in the schools.* Third edition. New York, NY: Merrily Publishing Co., pp. 238–239.

CHAPTER 3

Censorship

CENSORSHIP is not a new concept—the word *censorship* was used in the Roman Empire. The office of the censor was used to regulate public morals and watch over public conduct in Roman times. Today, censorship is a delicate issue. Sometimes it means removing books that disagree with the political views of the community and school board from school library shelves.

A recent article in California noted that in one year in the 1990s, 150 school districts experienced challenges to materials used by teachers or available in the school library. The ability to handle such a sensitive issue can make the difference in a principal surviving or not surviving his or her first few years. It takes only one major mishandled incident to place the principal in a vulnerable position. The main skills from the skill matrix include numbers 14 and 15, both of which involve understanding the community and knowing how to encourage involvement by groups outside the school community. These are both skills of socialization that are largely acquired by experience in working with groups of various political and religious persuasions. Those principals who are most able to handle these incidents have met many people, are comfortable with people, and are sensitive to the beliefs of the political right, left, and center.

A few of the books that have been removed from schools include: *Charlotte's Web, To Kill a Mockingbird, Brave New World, Black Like Me, The Adventures of Sherlock Holmes, The Good Earth, The Wizard of Oz,* and *Little Black Sambo.*

Court decisions have upheld the rights of school boards to remove books. The courts have also ruled that First Amendment rights should be upheld and that it is unconstitutional to remove books based upon the political tastes of school board members.

Relevant Skills

7. Awareness of the state code
12. Knowing where the ethical limits exist
14. Developing interpersonal networking skills
15. Knowing how to encourage involvement by all parties
20. Having a vision along with knowledge of how to achieve it
21. Desiring to make a difference in the lives of staff and students
23. Understanding that change is ongoing
24. Knowing how to assess job responsibilities

The United States Supreme Court considered its first school library book banning case in 1982. The censorship case involved the removal of nine books from the library shelves of the Island Trees Union School District. The school board defended its book removal by claiming that the books contained ''material which is offensive to Christians, Jews, Blacks and Americans in general,'' as well as ''obscenities, blasphemies, brutality, and perversion beyond description.'' After the school board's decision, Steven Pico and four other high school students sued the school district claiming that the board based its decision solely on a list of objectionable books published by a conservative parents' group.

The Court felt that the school board was attempting to deny students the right to hear ideas that may be contrary to those held by board members and ruled that the school library should be a receptacle for ideas from all persuasions.

The Pico decision supported school board influence in curriculum matters; however, that influence should not extend into the library, where voluntary inquiry is paramount.

The skills involved in the rubric of ''censorship'' are related to understanding the nature of censorship in American schools, being aware of the history of censorship, and knowing the types of recent incidents that have occurred, as well as their resolution. A knowledge of the geographical distribution of occurrences of censorship is also helpful.

The following case is not unlike many that might be faced by the new principal. This type of case reaches the media very quickly and might be a ''career breaker'' for the unaware administrator.

THE POEM

The Situation

Kent Mayfield was in his second year as middle school principal in the Andersonville School District in Middlefield, Minnesota. As he sat in his office on Friday at 4:00 P.M., he felt two strong emotions. One, he was relieved that his week was over. Two, confusion and wonderment were swirling through his head as he contemplated how he had gotten into this predicament.

He stared at the poem, taken from the eighth-grade test book, on his desk:

> *Freedom*
>
> *Shake off all that binds you*
> *Move your hands, they are free*
> *Move your lips, they are free*
> *Free to be, you and me,*
> *Unbound by the yoke of those who*
> *Bore thee*
> *Your body free . . .*

What to do? What to do? Mrs. Campbell and Mrs. Hopkins, mothers of eighth graders Dana and Marion, respectively, had just visited with him for an hour. Both protested that the poem encouraged ''free love'' and children to rebel against their parents. Both women were very influential in the local church and stated that ''filth like this'' was ruining the nation's youth. This was a state-mandated test, and Kent did not know of any other protests over this poem. He also thought he had convinced the parents to let the incident go since the test was over and a ''thing best left to the past.'' When they left, they cordially shook hands with Kent and stated that they knew ''he wasn't instrumental'' in developing the poem and the test in the first place and that they should all work to get rid of those who encouraged this ''secular humanist'' way of wrong thinking. They wanted to have the offensive poem removed immediately from the state test booklet, and they also wanted the principal to acknowledge that this was an offensive poem.

Kent felt that the best course for right now was to get more information. His first conversation with the superintendent last year, right after he was hired, really showed him that he must not make waves. After an uneventful first year on the job, he felt that all the warnings he had heard and admonishments to "be careful" of mine fields were so many words. His first conversation with Martin Enderly, the superintendent, ended with the superintendent warning: "Don't let any problems occur in your school that you can't handle there." The words did not concern him too much—especially considering that the school district had five elementary schools, one middle school, and one high school. It did not seem that such a small school district in a suburban/rural area could generate much controversy. Martin was known for his aversion to controversy, and every one of the other principals knew that it was best to try to solve any problems at the school site without sending them up to the superintendent or the school board. More than one principal in the past had not heeded this message and was no longer employed in the district. Martin had been superintendent for the past twelve years.

As Kent sat and pondered the issue, his thoughts reverted to three years ago when he was serving as a middle school assistant principal. At issue was a famous picture book that featured a naked boy on the front cover. The school librarian, Mrs. Witchett, had taken a black magic marker (yes, he remembered the black marker) and drawn boxer shorts to cover the boy's nakedness. In this case, a parent uproar ensued because the parents felt that censorship was being used against their wishes. What a battle! A parent group had formed to resolve the situation, and eventually the book (a new unadorned copy) was placed in a special reserve file in the back of the library workroom so that students could check it out with a parent present. He had learned from this lesson that the issue of censorship could go either way and that parents could easily be vociferous either for or against censorship. Would it help him in this situation?

Kent decided that his best course of action was to call in the eighth-grade teacher, Mrs. Morgan, and ask about the parents and their influence on school policy. After checking with his secretary, Mrs. Mosley, Kent learned that both parents had acted as gadflies in the past and nothing had ever come of any of the issues they had raised.

Monday Morning 7:30 A.M.

Kent asked Mrs. Morgan to come to his office. He came to the point immediately. "What do you know about Mrs. Hopkins and Mrs. Campbell? Have they ever complained about any books or poems, or any other issues?" Mrs. Morgan, a bright, small-boned, fortyish woman answered, "Oh, don't worry about them. They have always been cooperative—even room mothers for one year. They are very good friends—active and popular in the church. They occasionally have had a concern about their daughters academically—but nothing you need to worry about! I wouldn't lose any sleep about the whole thing! And you know that Martin likes to run a tight and QUIET ship!"

Kent suddenly felt relieved. After Mrs. Morgan had returned to class, he took out the poem again. What were Mrs. Campbell's and Mrs. Hopkins's concerns? That the poem encouraged free love? That the poem encouraged children to ignore their parents' concerns and care? Ridiculous! To him, the poem meant expressing your creativity, trying to see issues from a new point of view, letting yourself feel new feelings . . . and there could be nothing wrong with that. He smiled, thinking back to his own junior high school years—yin and yang, up and down, feeling fettered and feeling free—what a time. . . .

He placed the papers back in the file and walked to the large, gray, district-issued three-drawer cabinet. There he filed the letter under: TESTING-CENSORSHIP—PAST ISSUES. He then walked out into the bright morning light and the sounds of a busy playground.

Next Week, Tuesday, 10:00 A.M., School Board Meeting Day, Kent's Office

Mrs. Mosley walked into Kent's office with that concerned look that he knew so well on her face.

"The superintendent's on the line and he wants to talk with you immediately."

Kent looked surprised, then pressed the lit incoming line button. "Martin, how's it goin'?"

"Kent, get in my office right away. There's a contingent of fifty parents who are going to roast you alive for not responding to an obscene poem in some test. What the hell happened? I need to see you right now. I am totally unaware of this, and it doesn't look good for you!"

What could Kent have done to have avoided this crisis?

Machiavelli

A prudent Prince, or principal in this case, should bring wise men into his council and give them free license to speak the truth. He should ask his advisors about the total issue, then make his own decision. The principal has sought and received the wise counsel of his secretary and eighth-grade teacher. They have indicated that these parents are gadflies and not to be heeded. This is good advice but the principal should proceed one step further.

In this case, the principal should play the part of the fox and let the superintendent know immediately that these parents are not worthy of interest. The principal should relate to the superintendent all the past instances where these parents have acted out of the ordinary. In addition, the principal should spread through a group of trusted parents the fact that these two parents are out to destroy his reputation and bring disgrace down upon the school. This is how the fox outwits the flock and emerges the victor.

Lincoln

In this case, I would like to draw an analogy. Kent is not the general of the army in this case, but a lieutenant. This case reminds me of my participation in the Civil War, where I was told by my general of problems at a date later than I would have liked. I could give advice that Kent should follow in this situation, but I fear that it is too late for him to bring success to this case.

Upon receiving the visits of the two mothers he should have immediately called his superintendent and told him the whole story. Perhaps the superintendent already has relevant policies in place. Other parents, community members, and others in the district may have to be assembled to deliberate upon this issue. It is too large an issue to be addressed by Kent alone.

STUDY QUESTIONS

(*1*) Was there ''one fatal mistake'' that Kent committed in this case?

(*2*) Are there any dangers in categorizing groups in the school environment too narrowly? Is there a danger in using labels such as rightists, liberals, conservatives, or book burners?

(*3*) Were the opinions of the secretary and the middle school teacher valid? Why or why not?

(*4*) How would you have handled the situation? Who would you have included in your discussions?

SUGGESTED READINGS

Arons, S. (1981). The crusade to ban books. *Education Digest,* 47(3):2–5.

Donelsen, K. (1987). Six statement/questions from the censors. *Phi Delta Kappan,* 69(3):208–214.

Evans, C. (1988). In defense of *Huckleberry Finn:* Antiracism motifs in *Huckleberry Finn* and a review of racial criticism in Twain's work. Unpublished doctoral dissertation, Rice University.

Fedler, P. (1991). School book selection and reconsidered policies for managing challenges to schoolbooks in Nebraska. Unpublished doctoral dissertation, University of Nebraska.

Johnson, C. L. (1994). *Stifled laughter: One woman's story about fighting censorship.* Golden, CO: Fulcrum Publishing.

Moore, K. (1988). *Influences of censorship challenges on state textbook adoption criteria which affect school curriculum.* University of the Pacific, Stockton, CA.

Oliver, A. O. (1993). The politics of textbook controversy: Parents' challenge of a reading series. Unpublished doctoral dissertation, University of Wisconsin.

CHAPTER 4

Sexual Harassment

RECENTLY the issue of sexual harassment has taken on new importance in our culture. It is no longer acceptable to make snide or improper comments regarding someone's body parts or to ''come on'' to someone in a sexual manner without consent. The great difficulty in coping with sexual harassment is that violations usually occur in private with no witnesses. In the school, sexual harassment may occur at several levels. Sexual harassment may occur child to child, staff to staff, staff to student, and supervisor to subordinate.

When sexual harassment occurs between two staff members, it usually involves the credibility of two highly respected employees. Resolution of any allegations is a difficult and time-consuming process. If the offended party is more believable than the defendant and no action is taken by the administration, a lawsuit could result. This is because a failure to act creates a hostile work environment under current legal standings.

As in all issues involving personnel, the critical skills of law, ethics, and an innate desire to improve the school are crucial to resolution. In most school personnel issues, an understanding of the law does not solve the problem of external school politics. The next scenario shows how parental desires may become very inflexible in a short period of time and restricts the focus of the solution. What the parent desires to happen either is not feasible, is illegal, or both.

THE CASE OF THE PREDATORY TEACHER

Pelican Bay School District is bounded by soft, rolling hills and cattle land. It could easily be described as a traditional, rural, small town — the kind immortalized in Norman Rockwell's paintings.

Relevant Skills

7. Awareness of the state code
12. Knowing where the ethical limits exist
21. Desiring to make a difference in the lives of staff and students

---

The major industry of the community is logging and lumbering. Though the industry has seen a decline in mill fortunes, it is still a major source of income for the community and a major employer in the district.

The school board is composed of five members elected at large by the community, and it consists of three men and two women. The two women board members are employees of the lumber mill, one board member is in partnership on a cattle ranch, the board chair is a member of an old, established family within the community and operates several sections of land as a wheat and cattle ranch. The fifth board member is the owner/operator of the only grocery store in town and is the only board who could be described as having any sense of management philosophy; the others seeming to operate in the affective domain.

The administration of the district consists of Ms. Upright the high school principal. Ms. Upright has been with Pelican Bay Schools for just two years. The elementary principal, Mrs. Howitzer, has been in the district for over thirty years and seemingly is knowledgeable about most of the people within a three-countywide area. Mr. Gilligan is a cousin of the elementary school principal and is extremely jealous of the high school principal and her success. He was a schoolmate of Ms. Upright and has always felt a sense of intense competition with her. Consequently, the elementary principal, Mrs. Howitzer, persists in spreading rumors about the high school and this contributes to a constant state of turmoil at the high school.

While the town has a post office, a grocery store, a drug store, and a fast-food drive-in, there is no restaurant. Medical service requires a twenty-mile drive to a larger community. As a result, the locals congregate at the local tavern for morning coffee and for beer after work. All matters of concern in the town are discussed in the tavern, given special embellishment and flavor, and passed on as ''God's True Gospel.'' The town takes much pride in the high school athletic teams, with the crown jewel of the athletic program being the boys' basketball teams. The "pep band" receives almost as much glory as the basketball teams.

Ms. Hammond, the music teacher, is in charge of the band program, the girls' volleyball team, and the entire music program at the high school. She has been in the district for five years and is tenured. Prior to finding a home of her own within the boundaries of the Pelican Bay School District, she boarded with a local family (the Gilligans). The Gilligans' freshman-class daughter is active in the music program. From all appearances, the Gilligans and Ms. Hammond were close friends, attending church, music concerts, sports events, and other family-oriented activities together.

In October, Mr. Gilligan visits the office of Ms. Upright, the high school principal, and confides that his daughter, Sue, will not be attending school — she is pregnant. Ms. Upright agrees to keep the information confidential. Two months later, Mr. Gilligan inquires about Sue returning to Pelican Bay High School. Upon being assured that reenrollment is entirely possible and after being informed of the legal obligations of the school, Mr. Gilligan reenrolls Sue.

Sue naturally becomes the hot topic at the tavern. Thus, Ms. Hammond learns of Sue's pregnancy and decides to counsel her. In the course of the session, she proceeds to berate Sue and threatens her with loss of grades, etc. Later, she writes a long letter to Sue, telling her how much she loves her, how "close" they once were, how deeply hurt she is about the pregnancy, and that she never knew that Sue was seeing "that boy." Mr. Gilligan is now in Ms. Upright's office demanding that Ms. Hammond be fired: "You'll never have made a worse enemy if you don't fire her."

What would you do? Is there cause for action? What action? What would Abraham Lincoln do? What would Machiavelli do?

Machiavelli

Hereditary principalities are the easiest of all kingdoms to keep. One must simply never upset long-established customs. If one has no excessive vices that would cause the people to turn against him or her, then usually it is possible to remain in a position of power for a long time. However, mixed principalities are difficult to keep and to hold. Those that would desire your position and status in life will conspire and use all available tools to topple your kingdom. Likewise, the leader cannot stay friends with those that placed him or her in power, as they can never be fully trusted nor satisfied. To retain your power and position, you must make friends with the populace.

A leader must never endanger the kingdom for the sake of one individual. Exterminate the teacher of music in order to preserve the leadership position in the kingdom. Begin rumors about the music teacher in order to destroy her reputation. Form alliances with the enemies of Mr. Gilligan. Plot to discredit the elementary principal by playing upon his jealousy of the high school. This will weaken the enemy and generate a situation of divide and conquer. Investigate the law. If the law is on your side, use the law to your advantage; if the law makes the case against the band teacher, then ignore the law and use charisma. Trouble traced to the position of the leader is to be avoided at all costs.

Lincoln

Be decisive but in good time and in good order. Build your base of power through broad alliances. If possible have the school board issue policies that strengthen your hand. If at all possible, compromise with Mr. Gilligan; compromise is not a sign of weakness or a lack of leadership. Do not sacrifice the entire school for the sake of one small part of the organization. Loyalty is often built on private conversation and a sense of organizational commitment. Mr. Gilligan will destroy himself through his own actions. People are not foolish; they will see what is true. Follow the law. If the law is on your side, use the law, but do not go outside of the law. People must be shown what is true. Communicate what is good for a school by articulating the vision.

STUDY QUESTIONS

(*1*) What is the nature of the school and community in question?

(*2*) From reading the situation is it possible to determine if any improprieties have occurred? What might they be or not be?

(*3*) What is the legal definition of sexual harassment? Can sexual harassment occur on levels other than teacher to student? Can it occur student to student or supervisor to teacher?

(*4*) If there is not enough evidence for sexual harassment, what is your planned course of action?

(*5*) Is a written reprimand justified? If so, for what offense?

(*6*) At what point should the school board be informed? What about Mr. Gilligan's threat?

(*7*) How might the dynamics of the community work to your advantage or disadvantage?

(*8*) How would the local school district's collective bargaining contract fit into the above situation?

(*9*) What does the Civil Rights Act of 1964, Title VII reference? Does this act have meaning for any of the questions involved?

(*10*) Does your district have any policies regarding teacher-student relationships? How is professionalism defined in your state's statutes?

(*11*) Does your state have a strong certificate revocation law? What does it say?

(*12*) If the facts of the case were substantiated and nothing was done, would it be cause for a tort liability in your state?

SUGGESTED READINGS

Alexander, K. and Alexander, D. (1985). *American public school law.* St. Paul, MN: West Publishing Co.

La Morte, M. (1992). *School law: Cases and concepts.* Boston, MA: Allyn & Bacon Publishing.

See Equal Employment Opportunity Commission, Title VII of the Civil Rights Act of 1964.

Thomas, G., Sperry, D. and Wasden, F. (1991). *The law and teacher employment.* St. Paul, MN: West Publishing Co., pp. 103–107.

Vidich, A. and Bensman, J. (1968). *Small town in mass society; class, power, and religion in a rural community.* Princeton, NJ: Princeton University Press.

CHAPTER 5

Staff Morale

ONE of the most difficult areas to maintain at a consistently high level is that elusive concept of "staff morale." Is it possible to have all teachers in a school—perhaps a high school—working in the same direction? What happens when a new principal is placed in charge of a group of high school teachers who have been divided for years? How does a high school principal bring a divided staff together? It is not uncommon for a new principal to encounter "delicate balances" of relationships that have been teetering for years. How the principal resolves these balances, and if they are ever fully resolved, is a decided challenge. The following case is of a new high school principal who encounters hostility while relatively new in the position.

THE ANONYMOUS NOTE

Pat Stewart was into her second year as principal of the Sandpiper High School. She had worked very hard to achieve her position. She knew that few women had achieved the position of high school principal, and she was determined to show that she was on top of the job. She would try her best to have the best test scores of any high school in the county. She would make sure that her teachers were able to use the latest technology and keep up with the most recent teaching advances. Her prior experience in another state that had mandated site-based school councils prepared her for the new challenges she faced. Being the task-oriented individual that she was, she dived headlong into the new tasks. She organized parents to help survey the community and appointed teachers to key oversight committees. As far as Pat was concerned, events were moving forward.

Relevant Skills

2. Knowing how to facilitate group meetings
10. Knowing how to delineate employee roles
14. Developing interpersonal networking skills
15. Knowing how to encourage involvement by all parties
21. Desiring to make a difference in the lives of students and staff

---

Both the school board and the superintendent seemed to be pleased with the progress that Pat had made in such a short amount of time. Prior to having Pat come on board, the school had had only one other principal in twenty-five years. Mr. Clark, her predecessor, had been known as a "strong, traditional leader." He protected the teachers from all criticism. He interfered very little in the curriculum decisions that the teachers made and generally allowed very little input from the community into school programs.

Returning to her office after a special education student assessment meeting, Pat turned her attention to the stack of mail on her desk. One envelope caught her attention immediately. It was unusual because it had no return address.

> You think that you can sashay into this school and change everything around here. Well, you had better watch out because the staff does not care for what you are doing. You are blind to the obvious because the staff does not care for what you are doing. You are blind to the obvious because the staff is afraid. Many parents are upset with the introduction of "values" into the curriculum. You think that just because you came from another state you can push us around. You had better stop because you have lots of enemies on the staff who are PRETENDING to be your friend. You had better stop before the teachers go to the school board.

While Pat was not immediately concerned, she decided to take a few moments to reflect upon what could have precipitated such an action and, more importantly, who could have sent such a threat. After she had thought this over, she called in her secretary, Mrs. Gonzalez, about the communication she had just received.

Mrs. Gonzalez spoke haltingly. "Well, you know there are many factions on this faculty. They don't even get along with each other—much less a new administrator! You know that you have changed many things around here. I know you send birthday cards to teachers, and I know that you spend a lot of time observing in their classrooms and talking about standards. But I hear a lot . . . and what I hear is real negative by a pretty good sized group . . . you know . . . the complainers, who've seen a lot come and go . . . I just don't know."

Pat thanked Mrs. Gonzalez and reflected on her attempts to take a faculty of fifty and meld them into a cohesive team. Yes, she had made some unpopular decisions, posting scores of all faculty on the bulletin board. But she had been sure to celebrate birthdays by sending cards and having monthly birthday breakfasts for all those who have birthdays during the month! What had happened to cause this hostility?

Slowly she began to feel anger, and as her anger boiled over, she planned her remarks for the faculty meeting that was to be held later that day.

4:00 P.M. That Same Day — The Faculty Meeting

Pat began, "Some of this faculty are not professional in their approaches to conflict. Believe me when I say that those of you that cannot cope with the new program will not remain with this district for very long. Those of you that believe that you do not have to adapt to the site-based management ideas will either change or be changed." Pat paused and looked around at the angry expressions. "Now I know some of you really don't understand the concept so I am sending several of you to a county workshop next week. I hope you come back invigorated with new energy and ready to tackle your job anew." With that, she dismissed the staff from the meeting.

Later in the month at the regularly scheduled meeting of the board of directors, Pat noticed that a large contingent of her teaching staff was present. When the agenda called for "items of concern from the floor," the president of the local teachers' union asked to speak. "The teachers of this district resent being treated in an unprofessional manner and further resent threats and intimidation." He paused for effect. "Further, we will cover these issues in the upcoming bargaining session." He turned to face the audience and cast a meaningful glance at the faculty of Sandpiper High School. After, he turned to the president of the board with a firm stare and took his seat.

After the board meeting, the board president and superintendent tried to talk with the union leader but made no progress in understanding his comments. The next day, the superintendent called Pat to her office. "Pat, we have a real problem here. I need to see you right away!"

You are Pat Stewart. How might Pat have improved communication early enough in her tenure to have avoided this crisis?

Machiavelli

No prince should mind being called cruel if it means keeping tight control over his subjects. This is the reputation that must be held no matter what the outcomes are. The principal in this case should have come in as the lion enters his lair. The principal should have immediately tried to dismiss one or two of the faculty just for the purpose of instilling fear in the hearts of the others. This action would have caused the others to be off balance and unwilling to risk their livelihoods to take on the principal. Enough with birthday cards and observing classes! Of course, the law of tenure may have defeated the prince in the end. The process of trying to eradicate part of this faculty is what would be remembered!

Lincoln

You must never shun conflict, but embrace it as soon as the slight tendrils appear on the stalk. If this principal had addressed—and addressed hard—the seeds of discontent at the start of her reign, she would have cut off many of the problems that she encounters now.

I remember as a youth I had a large field in which I had to set up my crops. This field had many tree stumps—some large and some small. The smaller ones I could root out with ease or perhaps burn out if they were larger. But the large stumps, I could not remove. There was no other way but to plough around these stumps. Pat should have met with individual members of the faculty early and often. She would have found those stumps that were too difficult to plough through and avoided them at all costs.

STUDY QUESTIONS

(*1*) How should Pat handle her meeting with the superintendent?

(*2*) Does she have anything to fear from this situation?

(*3*) What do you surmise is behind the union involvement?

(*4*) What can you guess is Pat's leadership style? Could the style have been formed by her past experiences?

(*5*) Suppose you are asked to be a consultant to assist in facilitation of site-based management at a high school site. What are you going to recommend, and where are you going to start?

(*6*) What evidence do we have that site-based management will improve a student's educational experience? What sources would you use to investigate this issue?

(*7*) Compare the advice of Machiavelli and Lincoln. How are they similar or different?

SUGGESTED READINGS

Hanson, M. (1993). *Educational leadership and organizational behavior.* Third edition. New York, NY: Allyn & Bacon Publishing.

Hersey, P. and Blanchard, K. (1993). *Management of organizational behavior.* Englewood Cliffs, NJ: Prentice-Hall.

CHAPTER 6

Communication

NO organizational change or improvement in student outcomes evolves without communication. The specific skills that are included from Table 1 (see Introduction) include knowing how to facilitate small and large group meetings, establishing a positive relationship with others, knowing how to communicate with authority when necessary, and communicating with parent and community groups. These are not all of the requisite skills, but it is difficult to proceed without them.

When individuals are selected to be principals of schools, they are asked many questions during the initial interview regarding student scheduling, custodial formulas, instructional objectives, curriculum reform, and school safety. It is very difficult to assess interpersonal skills such as communication in two or three interviews. Some districts have tried "in-basket" exercises or other methods to get around this problem.

The following case illustrates the fact that sometimes a principal's personal inclinations and skills can interfere with running the school well. The case illustrates clearly what may happen if skills and abilities are not constantly assessed and weaknesses improved upon. Of these skills, communication may be regarded as one of the most important.

THE QUIET ONE

Jan Parker called the faculty meeting to order. This was her second year at the Helmsley K−6 school, and even though it was difficult for her, she would once more try to educate the faculty in the latest curriculum reforms.

"Now, who has read Dr. Michael's book, *Curriculum: The Year 2000?*" From the group of fifteen teachers, only Mary, a quiet sixth-grade teacher hesitantly raised her hand, looking sheepishly around at the other teachers as she did so.

33

Relevant Skills

2. Knowing how to facilitate group meetings
9. Establishing a positive relationship with other administrators
11. Knowing how to relate to school board members
15. Knowing how to encourage involvement by all parties
17. Knowing organizational power and authority

"I can't believe that Mary is the only one who has read this book! Here we have a book reading only once every month! I have provided half a dozen copies of our book-of-the-month selection in the library, and usually only one or two of you read the selection! Well, we'll try again next month. Our next agenda item is about the Xerox machine breaking down again, and I bet everyone has an opinion on that!" As she saw the suddenly interested expressions, she knew she was right again! Back to the drawing board.

Later That Afternoon in Her Office

Jan slipped back to her office around 5:00 P.M. after the meeting. She glanced at the pile of mail to be opened and decided it would be best to load it into a cardboard box and open it later. She reflected on her past and how it might have affected her love for curriculum reform and leading others to change their teaching.

Jan had been a quiet, studious "bookworm" as a child. She thought that no better afternoon could be spent than to open another mystery or biography from the town library. (She had read all the books in the elementary school library by the eighth grade.) School had been easy for her — even graduate school — and she naturally had become a sixth-grade teacher partly because of her love for education.

But after five years of teaching, she began to see that other teachers did not try to learn new teaching techniques. They still brought out the same old lesson plans and did not pay attention to state frameworks or new suggestions for improvement. Although these teachers were the minority of most staffs, it disturbed Jan that not more were "up on things."

Jan decided to go back to graduate school and obtain her certificate to become an administrator. She landed a job as an assistant principal. Then, when Mrs. Alvarez left Helmsley to take a middle school principalship, Jan was selected by the superintendent, Dr. Brown, because Helmsley needed "someone to develop the staff, curriculum-wise." In other words, Helmsley needed a little shaking up. The test scores were down, and the staff development funds were scarce. Therefore, Dr. Brown directed Jan to create her own staff development opportunities. He would be able to provide some funding if needed — but not much.

Jan studied with a vengeance all the curriculum reforms she could. Every morning from 9:00 A.M. to 11:00 A.M., she locked herself in her office and reviewed every state framework in use. She asked faculty members to report on recent books at meetings. She assigned Mr. Brown, her assistant principal, the tasks of meeting with teachers, handling discipline problems, and dealing with budget and custodial issues. Jan even stopped creating the weekly newsletter to parents that Mrs. Alvarez had done so well. Instead, she sent parents a monthly book review. Her total concentration was on educating her staff on the latest educational reforms.

Boy, Jim Brown had been a real help! He was there from early in the morning to late at night to take on the tasks of meeting parents, holding conferences with teachers and students, handling discipline problems, and otherwise making himself indispensable to the staff. Jan really appreciated his presence and his constant willingness to help. He may not know every curriculum reference as Jan did, but he knew how to get the plumbing unstopped in the girl's restroom faster than anyone, including the custodian.

Even though Jan held the monthly faculty/literary meetings, Jim held the weekly faculty/parent meetings that ironed out the many pesky problems that cropped up on categorical budgeting, busy schedules, and choice of teachers.

Jan thought about Jim's communication skills. Unlike her, he enjoyed being surrounded by staff and students. He knew everyone's name in the whole school. He called out their names on the playground. He sent birthday cards to all the teachers. He didn't read the monthly journals. He hated regular weekly meetings, but he attended all the birthday parties, all the weddings, and all the funerals. The parents knew him, too. How could she have known? He didn't tell her. . . .

Wednesday Morning 9:00 A.M.

Jan's secretary called into her office: "Dr. Hendricks is on the line for you, Jan." Jan lifted the receiver with trepidation. She knew that the superintendent only called when there was a major problem.

"Jan, we have a problem here. We have a list of 500 parent names from your school on a petition requesting that you be transferred, or worse, that your assistant principal, Jim Brown, take over immediately as principal. The petition people, signers, whatever, say that you don't communicate at all with students, teachers, or parents and that you make your staff read these dumb books all day. They say that this takes them away from working with students. We have a real problem here, Jan. This is signed by every one of your teachers except one, I believe her name is Mary. You better get over here right away! We may have to take a hard look at this!"

What can Jan do to handle this situation?

Machiavelli

There are those who aspire to princely power by criminal or evil conduct. This occurred when Agathocles, a Sicilian, became prince of Syracuse. Born the son of a potter, he joined the military and used all sorts of villainy to assume this position. So, indeed, did Jim Brown. He deliberately assumed those duties that the principal did not take on. He ingratiated himself with students, parents, and teachers.

Jan did not heed his actions. Her attention was directed to activities that did not protect her territory. It is too late for her to recoup her losses. She did not communicate well to those around her and wasted her time with useless literary pursuits instead of guarding her territory.

Lincoln

I could not direct my armies as I did and talk to my generals without clear, direct, and frequent communication. I needed to articulate and define for others, even in my early law practice, what might have remained unsaid. I always needed to influence those around me by communication.

I do not see how Jan was chosen for this appointment. It appears to me that she was not well-suited for this position. It reminds me of my search for the "perfect" general. I found that many of my generals refused to fight for me, and it took many years and many false starts before I found my perfect general—General Ulysses S. Grant. He directed his troops with clarity and compassion. I communicated well with him also. Before I met with Ulysses to give him direction, I wrote out my instructions. After talking with him, I adjusted these instructions based upon his words and gave him the instructions for the purpose of later contemplation. In this way, he had my words personally and in writing.

My advice to Jan is to ask for a period of time to turn her staff around. I would also be careful that my assistant principal was working as an assistant rather than as the leader of the organization. I prided myself on spending more time with my troops than back in Washington among the wolves who were always circling and plotting to take over my job!

STUDY QUESTIONS

(*1*) Should Jan have adjusted her leadership style to the sophistication of the teachers in her school? Why or why not?

(*2*) How might Jan have assessed her mistakes earlier in her career?

(*3*) Is there anything Jan could have done to avert the crisis?

SUGGESTED READINGS

Braden, W. W. (1988). *Abraham Lincoln: Public speaker.* Baton Rouge, LA: University Press.

Burns, J. M. (1978). *Leadership.* New York, NY: Harper and Row.

CHAPTER 7

Managing Resources

WITH many district managers of resources being "downsized" out of the district office, it has become more important for the principal to know how to manage funds. This involves the skills of analysis, data gathering, personnel management, and tracking. In this age, almost no decision about managing school resources is made without the involvement of many people.

The following case study is a classic, as it leads a novice principal to a trap not necessarily of his or her own making. What begins as a very positive experience degenerates into a problem situation that may sink a short career.

THE LOTTERY

Mark Adamson walked into the principal's meeting one early October Monday morning amid a happy buzz of excited talk. This was the first meeting in October and the first meeting in which he thought some "up" topics would be discussed. As Mark sat down, he noticed that the superintendent, Joe Martin, would be conducting the meeting rather than the assistant superintendent. This usually meant *good* news.

The meeting was called to order, and the good news was announced first. "Every school will be allotted lottery monies according to enroll-ment," Joe announced proudly. "The money should be sent to you in May, and how it is spent is totally up to you."

One of the principals raised his hand. "Are we sure that this money is forthcoming? We really have not received money as promised in the past."

The superintendent responded, "There is no chance that this money will be held up. This is good news for all of us."

Relevant Skills

2. Knowing how to facilitate group meetings
3. Knowing how to design a data-based improvement process
4. Knowing how to develop and monitor a budget
6. Knowing how to establish a scheduling system
8. Knowing how to manage operational services

The remainder of the meeting passed quickly for Mark. He couldn't wait to get back to the school to start dividing up that money!

One Week Later

Mark announced to the faculty that he had appointed a committee of two teachers and four community members to divide up the $65,200 in lottery funds. He set the dates of the meetings and wished the group luck. The only ground rules were that the group needed to come to consensus on all priority decisions. In addition, all expenditures were to be allotted to classrooms and must benefit all students in the school. The group would meet for two hours every week with a facilitator and an assigned group leader.

One Month Later

Mark waited in his office for the leader of the priority group, Mrs. Shattuck. She was the parent selected to present to him the final lottery list. Mark was very pleased. He had heard that the group had done a super job in allotting lottery funds. Most of the money was assigned for computers, software, and computer training for the staff.

Mrs. Shattuck met with Mark and expressed her thanks for his help in the process. She was pleased that the group had done such a good job in prioritizing—so pleased, in fact, that she had just given an interview to the local newspaper.

February 1

The atmosphere at the principals' meeting was somber. None of the principals knew what the assistant superintendent was going to say, but they knew it was not good news. They did not wait long. The assistant superintendent announced the following: "It pains me to tell all of you that the lottery funds must be used this year to balance the budget. Other funds have not been received by the district, and this is a necessity. I know that this change is an inconvenience to you, and so for this I am sorry.''

The Board Meeting

Mrs. Shattuck addressed the board of education: ''We, of the Holmes School, are requesting that the principal, Mark Adamson, be removed from office because of our lack of confidence in his ability. He told us we had $65,000 and now we don't. What happened to this money? We don't understand. We just know he did not tell us the truth and now we want him gone.''

Mark's stomach tightened as he studied the faces of the board members. What was going to happen? What had gone wrong?

Machiavelli

There are some cases where the leader must back down from assuming total responsibility for a grievous error. In this case Mark should quickly place all blame upon the superintendent, Joe Martin. In this way he will be offensively addressing the concerns of Mrs. Shattuck and directing the board's wrath to the place it should be directed — the superintendent. This of course must be done carefully and behind the scenes. It would not bode well for Mark to be seen carrying out this plan. A compatriot working for Mark would be of great use here.

Lincoln

This is a case where Mark should address the board fair and square and explain the circumstances fully. He should fully admit his error. In reality the superintendent was at fault for being overly optimistic regarding the receipt of these funds. The superintendent should have expressed cautious hope that these funds would be received.

STUDY QUESTIONS

(*1*) Who made the original mistake? What was the original mistake?
(*2*) What might Mark have done differently? Did emotion enter into his actions?

(*3*) What does this case demonstrate about the nature of lottery funds?

(*4*) Should you use a community/teacher group to prioritize any new funds to the school?

(*5*) Should the assistant superintendent announce the bad news? Why or why not?

SUGGESTED READINGS

Burrup, P. E., Brimley, V. and Garfield, R. R. (1993). *Financing education in a climate of change.* Needham Heights, MA: Simon and Schuster.

Calonius, E. (1991). The big payoff from lotteries, *Fortune,* March 25, p. 109.

Cetron, M. J. and M. E. Gayle. (1990). Educational renaissance: 43 trends for U.S. schools. *The Futurist,* pp. 34, 37.

Schmieder, J. H. and Townley, A. J. (1994). *School finance: A California perspective.* Dubuque, IA: Kendall Hunt Publishing.

CHAPTER 8

Conflict Management

CONFLICT occurs daily and often on an hourly basis within the public schools. The sources of conflict are as varied as the issues that a pluralistic society engenders.

While the sources of conflict may vary, conflict itself may be categorized according to whether it is interpersonal, intrapersonal, intergroup, intragroup, or interorganizational. When we combine these categories with what we know about leadership styles, personality traits, and communication styles, then we can develop strategies for learning how to cope with conflict.

Frequently, beginning administrators accelerate organizational conflict by acting out of haste, not analyzing the situations, failing to perform a force-field analysis, or miscommunicating their actions. Miscommunications can be acerbated by the leader when the leader does not understand his or her own leadership style or the impact that a particular style may have on others. The leader's style of communication must be appropriate to the maturity level of the followers and the situational elements of the organization.

This scenario is designed to give students the opportunity to examine their leadership styles and communications styles.

THE CASE OF HARRY AND SALLY

Harry and Sally Smith have been employed by the Riverview School as custodians for fifteen years. Harry is the day custodian and Sally's immediate supervisor. As such, he is responsible for the hiring, firing, discipline, transfer, and evaluations (both formative and summative). Sally works the night shift and is responsible for the general cleaning of the building. This includes sweeping, dusting, emptying of the trash cans, and mopping and buffing of the halls and multipurpose (MP) room.

43

Relevant Skills

2. Knowing how to facilitate group meetings
5. Knowing how to conduct parent-teacher-student conferences
8. Knowing how to manage operational services
11. Knowing how to relate to school board members

Harry, who works days is in charge of the boiler room, general repair, setup and breakdown of lunch tables in the MP room, and arrangement of chairs for plays, concerts, parent gatherings, etc.

Sally is a member of the bargaining unit as defined in the contract, but Harry is not. The bargaining contract has "just cause" for dismissal included in the agreement.

David Beatle had been the elementary principal of Riverview for over twenty-five years. David often referred to Riverview as a happy family. For the last fifteen years, David had signed, but not authored, the evaluations for both Harry and Sally. Harry has been the sole author of Sally's evaluation. Sally's best friend is the building secretary, Sue.

David Beatle is proud of the fact that the building looks good. He also likes to brag about how he has never had to hire substitute custodians for his building from the district substitute pool. It is also true that his building had the lowest cost per pupil for support services in the district. The school board is aware of this situation and made plans to inform the community of the fine tax savings under David's leadership.

Unbeknownst to Dr. Letterman, the district superintendent, David had allowed Harry to substitute for Sally whenever Sally was ill, had doctor appointments, or any other obligations that might interfere with Sally's inalienable right to "pursue happiness."

This arrangement was discovered by Dr. Letterman during the second year of his tenure in the district. In the fall of the second year, two changes in personnel occurred. Harry had open heart surgery, divorced Sally, and subsequently retired before the end of October.

Dr. Letterman reviewed the district policy on hiring new support personnel, advertised, interviewed, and selected a replacement. While Sally was an applicant within the pool, she was not selected. The new head custodian at Riverview was young and very much interested in making Riverview "shine like tomorrow."

In a related move, David Beatle retired during the summer and still resides inside the school district, visiting his friends on the school board and the superintendent regularly. He often brags "how great things were with Harry and Sally 'in the good old days.' "

Two months after the appointment of the new head custodian, Sally began to have problems meeting her work schedule. George discovered this situation through a chance meeting with the new head custodian.

"How is it going in the new position?" George Young asked in passing. The reply was less than what he thought he should receive when the new head custodian responded by saying, "I can't do all of my day work and do half of Sally's too! I've talked to her about pulling her weight, but nothing has happened! I'm about ready to quit on the whole thing!"

Upon further investigation, George learns that Sally has been leaving work early and leaving a lot of the night work for the head custodian. "Why have you not begun progressive discipline on Sally?" asks George Young.

"Because I was told that we work as family in this building. You know that as well as I do. We all pitch in when one person falls behind, even if it means working longer hours," responded the new head custodian.

"Well, I can't explore this much more today with you. I have to attend a meeting of the long-range planning committee now, but we will meet again after I get back from the American Association of School Administrators meeting in Florida next week."

Upon George Young's return, he finds the following items awaiting.

(*1*) A grievance from Sally claiming a violation of past practice standards

(*2*) A workers' compensation claim filed by Sally, for an alleged fall the day after George's conversation with the head custodian

(*3*) A visit from a board member and Dr. Letterman, who want to know why Sally is being harassed

You are George. Where do you begin to unravel the issues?

Machiavelli

When you are close to the kingdom and live there, it is easier to see troubles coming and take care of them right away. When the leader is absent, problems grow and become more difficult to manage and solutions are not as easy to come by. One needs plenty of luck and resolution to hold onto new territories. You must be ruthless in stamping out disloyalty to the kingdom! Remember, it is better to be feared than to be loved. When establishing a presence in new kingdoms, it is better to stamp out the old lines. In this way, power may be consolidated. Fire the new head custodian as he is expendable. Bide your time so that you may replace David Beatle. He, too, must go as he is not tough enough. Others are running the building, not him! Look for ways to deflect all criticism from yourself.

Lincoln

It is better to be respected and loved, than to be feared. Never act out of vengeance, but only out of kindness. Remember, followers in virtually every organization respond better to empathy and compassion. It is impolitic to crush a man and make him your enemy. Visit with Sally and her supervisor. Try to find common ground. Adjust the schedule so that Sally may come in earlier and doesn't have to leave as late.

STUDY QUESTIONS

(*1*) What theories of organizational behavior are in place here?

(*2*) What is the role of David Beatle in creating this situation?

(*3*) Classical theory argues that tight organizational structure is the only way to achieve goals. Social systems theory argues that the way to effectiveness is to allow people to become empowered. In the above situation, what is the relationship between the two?

(*4*) What does situational leadership call for in this scenario?

(*5*) Are there issues of law at stake? What are the elements of ''just cause'' in a dismissal case?

(*6*) Examine your leadership style. How does it fit into the picture?

(*7*) What are the moral and ethical implications here? Ethics is the study of what is good and beautiful. Do you see any need for administrators to sort out their individual philosophies? Why or why not?

(*8*) How should the board member be handled? Is there an easy solution?

(*9*) How does your district protect itself against fraudulent workers' compensation claims?

(*10*) Who do you suspect of tipping off the board member? David Beatle or Sally? Who gains? Who loses?

(*11*) How might Sue play a role in all of this?

(*12*) Why fire the new head custodian? What legal problems might occur in that action?

(*13*) What is meant by the term "constructive discharge"? What are your state laws regarding "property interests" to employment? Might anyone have claim here?

(*14*) Providing George Young works through this problem, what information does he have to bear in mind from now on? Who would you list as people he needs to be on the lookout for?

SUGGESTED READINGS

Barge, K. (1994). *Leadership: Communication skills for organizations and groups.* New York, NY: St. Martin's Press.

Berne, Eric, (1964). *Games people play.* New York, NY: Grove Press.

Bondesio, M. (August, 1992). Conflict management at school: An unavoidable task. Paper presented at the meeting of the Society for Regional Conference of the Commonwealth Council for Education Administration, Hong Kong.

Earnest, G. et al. (1993). Styles as reflections of Jungian personality type preferences of cooperative extension's north central region directors and district directors. (Research report No. SR 71). Columbus, Ohio, Ohio State University, Department of Agricultural Education.

Fisher, W. and Koue, G. (1991). Conflict management. *Library Administration and Management,* 5(3):145−146, 148−150.

Gemelch, Walter and Carroll, James. (1991). The three Rs of conflict management for department chairs and faculty. *Innovative Higher Education,* 18(3):107−123.

Glasser, Wm. (1994). *The control theory manager.* New York, NY: Harper Collins Publishers, Inc.

Hanson, M. (1991). *Educational administration and organizational behavior.* Needham Heights, MA: Allyn & Bacon Publishing.

Hartley, M. (1985). Leadership style and conflict resolution: No man(ager) is an island. *Journal of Cooperative Education,* 21(2):16−23.

Hersey, P. and Blanchard, K. (1993). *Management of organizational behavior: Utilizing human resources.* Sixth edition. Englewood Cliffs, NJ: Prentice-Hall.

McGuire, J. (1984). Strategies of school district conflict. *Sociology of Education,* 57(1):31−42.

Monroe, C. et al. (1989). Conflict behaviors of difficult subordinates. *Southern Communication Journal,* 54(4):311−329.

Morrill, C. and Thomas, C. (1992). Organizational conflict management as disputing process: The problem of social escalation. *Human Communication Research*, 18(3):400−428.

Personnel policy book of the district in which you work.

Wheeless, L. and Reichel, L. (1990). A reinforcement model of the relationship of supervisors' general communication styles and conflict management styles to task attraction. *Communication Quarterly*, 38(4):372−387.

Zuelke, D. and Willerman, M. (1992). *Conflict and decision making in elementary schools*. Dubuque, IA: Wm. C. Brown Publishing Inc.

CHAPTER 9

Community Involvement and Awareness

KNOWING a community and that community's values, is directly related to an administrator's ability to foster change. The ability of a principal to diagnose a community environment rapidly and accurately, is crucial to the change process and the school's mission. Sensing when to change the organizational culture is often more important than the change itself. Possessing the skills associated with change strategies will assist the school administrator in managing the conflict that change generates while engendering a culture of excellence. When the culture of a school is modified to accept high standards of self-discipline and academic achievement for its students, then the educational mission of the school is more easily fulfilled. Generating excellence in a school system depends on the instructional leader being able to promote incremental change relative to the political environment.

The astute student of school leadership theory will recognize that effective leadership is a function of the leader's style, personality, skill, and ability to articulate a vision acceptable to the followers in a particular political situation. How the political situation impacts a particular school is often dictated by community demographics. Ultimately, the success or failure of the school leader depends on the degree of community homogeneity/heterogeneity, intensity of political activity, and the decision-making style of the local board of directors.

When the principal's leadership style is included in the equation, then the change process becomes even more complex. The leader of a large urban school will interact differently with the various factions than will the leader of a small rural school. Therefore, the change processes are not always the same. Small rural schools are often at the sacred end of the change continuum, while the larger, more urban schools reflect a secular viewpoint.

Relevant Skills

2. Knowing how to facilitate group meetings
14. Developing interpersonal networking skills
15. Knowing how to encourage involvement by all parties
16. Maintaining positive relationships with other agencies
19. Portraying self-confidence on the job
22. Being aware of one's biases, strengths, and weaknesses

Communities with a more secular outlook seek change for the sake of change. This is the educational equivalent of keeping up with the Joneses. On the other hand, sacred communities resist change, because of their inherent mistrust of moving away from the familiar. Knowing where a school falls on the change continuum is critical to the ongoing school-improvement process. The following exercise is designed to facilitate and understand the process of change in a complex society.

THE JOHN JAY RUSSELL SCHOOL DISTRICT

The John Jay Russell School District is located on the outskirts of a large, highly popular recreational area. The attendance area draws in 5,000 students in grades K−12. The student body is diverse and includes a mix of rural and town students. There are some children of federal employees who live adjacent to the popular recreational/wilderness area and a number of students from a large alternative religious group.

The year-round population of the town of Russell is relatively small (5,000) but during the summer, the population swells to over 10,000 people. Many of the summer residents are young people who spend much of their spare time in the wilderness area. Permanent residents are mostly seasonal employees who accommodate the influx of tourists during the summer months. Off season, many permanent residents spend a great deal of time lounging in the local taverns and collecting unemployment checks. Other residents of the area make their living outfitting city folks for the backcountry. During the last five years, the population has begun to grow because of the town's proximity to prime recreational land, its natural beauty, and its access to wildlife. A building boom is in progress. Additionally, a ''new-age'' religious group has established a large commune inside the school district's attendance boundaries.

Eight years ago, the community of Russell experienced a significant challenge to its educational system when the high school burned to the ground. Only a few trophies from the trophy case were salvaged. The new school was built with a combination of funds from the federal government, insurance claims, and a local bond issue. The project generated a sense of community and pride in the local schools. Likewise, Mr. Olsen, the superintendent, gained the respect and admiration of Russell citizens as a quality leader of the community and its school.

While the dollar amount spent per pupil is among the highest in the state, the support of the community has always been strong. Mr. Olsen enjoys one of the highest salaries of any school superintendent in the state and is highly regarded by his peers. The teaching staff is diverse, and most teachers stay until retirement. By contrast, the high school principal position seems to become vacant every two to three years.

The John Jay Russell School District is experiencing problems that never used to occur, except in larger more urban school systems. Drug, alcohol, and tobacco use is increasing among the student population. Several students have been caught with guns in their possession and several fist fights have occurred on the school grounds. It is the issue of discipline that has caused the most controversy.

One new school board member, who recently defeated an incumbent, has openly criticized the administration at the high school for ''being too harsh on the students.'' Other members of the board are demanding a crackdown on what is viewed as ''lawless behavior.'' Most of the discipline problems stem from the students that reside in the commune and from students who have recently moved into the school district from more urban areas. A proposed solution has been to set up a school within the boundaries of the alternative religious compound. That has been answered by the threat of a lawsuit by the parents of the affected students. More recently, letters to the editor of the local paper have begun to appear critical of the district's handling of the matter. An incumbent school board member has been defeated at the polls by a challenger from the community.

You are the high school principal of Russell High. How would you solve the problems of discipline?

Machiavelli

The power of a prince stems from either the power of the people or the power of the nobles, depending upon which group has the better chance to prevail. When the nobles feel threatened by the power of the people, they will build up their power through one of their own. Likewise, when the people feel threatened by the power of the nobles, they promote one of their own and use his authority as a shield. Attaining power through the nobles makes it more difficult for the prince to retain power. This is due to the fact that the prince is surrounded by many who see themselves as equals, making it difficult to give orders or manage his affairs as he sees fit. You cannot satisfy the nobles, but you can satisfy the people, as the aim of the commoner is more honest than that of the nobles. The worst that a hostile populace can do to a prince is abandon him. Hostile nobles will not only abandon the prince but also attack him directly.

Ignore the advice of the nobles as they represent the power of the past. Concentrate instead on the power of the people and do their bidding. In this way, you may be able to retain your position of power and influence, provided that you take pains to insulate yourself from the wrath of the nobles.

Lincoln

Garnering public support is crucial to the success of any endeavor that will solve the problems presented here. Without the support of the public, no solution will succeed. It is up to the leader to mold public sentiment by providing accurate information on the issues. This may be accomplished only through an honest and forthright manner. Do not try to coerce the situation. Coercion forces confrontation through the use of dictatorial powers while abandoning the leadership element. People truly want to feel that the decisions will make a difference.

Form a committee to analyze the difficulties and the causes of the current conflict. Have the committee forward recommendations to you regarding all potential solutions from which you will select the best and send them to the board of directors for their approval, rejection, or modification. This procedure allows the board members to remain in the position of policy makers and preserves their role and yours while you continue to provide the leadership element.

Develop a school newsletter to the parents of the school. Outline what the research says about safe schools. In the newsletter, reveal the incidences of violence that have occurred, the number of minor but repeated violations of school discipline policy, etc. In this manner, the public at large will become aware of the need to develop a plan of action in support of your ideas. Generate speaking engagements to the local service clubs in order to get the message out.

STUDY QUESTIONS

(*1*) What do you see as the pros and cons of the advice given by Lincoln and Machiavelli?

(*2*) To what degree has the change in the community precipitated the crisis in this school?

(*3*) What style of leadership is being suggested in the advice given by Lincoln? What is being suggested by Machiavelli?

(*4*) Is the community in the above scenario sacred or secular in nature? What evidence might support your conclusions?

(*5*) Why is it important for building-level administrators to understand the nature of a community?

(*6*) What are the three things that every administrator should monitor as communities change?

SUGGESTED READINGS

Bailey, F. G. (1965). Decisions by consensus in councils and committees: With specific reference to village and local government of India. In M. Banton (ed.). *Political system and the distribution of power.* Columbus, OH: Frederich A. Prager Publishers, pp. 1−20.

Hersey, P. and Blanchard, K. (1993). *Management of organizational behavior: Utilizing human resources.* Fifth edition. Englewood Cliffs, NJ: Prentice-Hall.

Hosman, C. (1990). Superintendent selection and dismissal: A changing community defines its values. *Urban Education,* 25(3):350−369.

Iannaconne, L. and Lutz, F. (1970). *Politics, power and policy: The governing of local school districts.* Columbus, OH: Charles E. Merrill.

Kerr, N. (1964). The school board as an agency of legitimation. *Sociology of Education,* 38:34−59.

Kirkendall, R. (1966). Discriminating social, economic, and political characteristics of changing versus stable policy making systems in school districts. Unpublished doctoral dissertation, Claremont Graduate School.

Lutz, F. and Iannaconne, L. (1978). *Public participation in local school districts.* Lexington, MA: D.C. Heath and Company.

Rada, R. (1989). A political context framework for the study of local school governance. Unpublished manuscript.

Roberts, W. (1990). *Leadership secrets of Attila the Hun.* New York, NY: Warner Press, Inc.

Sharpe, D. (1984). *Choosing leadership styles.* Montana State University Extension Service Bulletin No. MT 8404.

Vidich, A. and Bensman, J. (1968). *Small town in mass society; class, power, and religion in a rural community.* Princeton, NJ: Princeton University Press.

Wirt, F. and Kirst, M. (1972). *The political web of American schools.* Boston, MA: Little, Brown and Co.

Wirt, F. and Kirst, M. (1982). *The politics of education: Schools in conflict.* Berkeley, CA: McCutchen Publishing Corporation.

Zeigler, H., Jennings, M. and Peak, W. (1974). *Governing American schools: Political interaction in local school districts.* North Sciuate, MA: Duxbury Press.

CHAPTER 10

Balancing a Personal Life

THE thirteenth critical skill is understanding how the principalship changes one's family and other personal relationships. One of the greatest challenges of a high school principal is balancing a personal life with the constant need to attend to the business of the high school. The business of the high school involves many night functions including parent meetings, basketball games, school dances, baseball games, and more sports.

Before taking on the role of high school principal, it is necessary to plan how to balance a personal life with a demanding and stressful professional life. This case is of a good man who tried to do a good job. As a young principal, he sought to spend many nights at the job. His personal life began to suffer and evolve into a crisis situation after his attention to his job became an obsession.

IS THAT LIQUOR ON HIS BREATH?

Jack Armstrong was the newest high school principal in a long line of principals at the Farley High School in Merriam, Montana. Merriam, Montana, was formed as a township in 1866 as a center of ranching and wheat farming. While the early years of the pioneer struggle are behind the town and modern communications have made their impact, the town still remains isolated from the mainstream of society, even by Montana standards.

Farley High School is a fairly small high school—400 students—but more active than most. The high school is the "only game in town" for most folks. The number of churches in town slightly exceeds the number of taverns—but not by much. The main recreation in the community

---

Relevant Skill

13. Understanding how the principalship changes one's family relationships

---

consists of Farley High football and basketball games, the yearly rodeo, and the annual wild horse auction.

Jack came from Bozeman two years ago with his wife Jane and three-year-old daughter Karen. He had been an active assistant principal and football coach at the "winningest high school in Bozeman" as it was called. The superintendent of the Merriam school district knew the value of a winning football team and emphasized in his hiring interview that this is what she wanted and she wanted it fast.

Jack worked very hard that first year. The majority of the faculty was behind him. He was perceptive enough to rely on Joan Mobley, his assistant vice principal, to deal with most of the instructional issues while he handled the community issues, night dances, and of course, sports activities with his football head coach Chuck Forester.

Chuck and Jack worked four nights out of the week to bring the team along. They held many practices – far more than had been held in the past two years. Chuck and Jack became fast friends and frequently drove into the next town, Larabee – thirty minutes away – to have a few beers after practice or after a game.

The community began to notice a change in the football team. It was winning more games. Its morale was higher. The team was no longer regarded as the "Farley Fraidycats" by other teams in the state. In fact, it was headed for the state playoffs that year.

Jack's wife, Jane, was noticing other things. She noticed that Jack was coming home later and later from games and practices. It was not unusual for him to return home after 1:00 A.M. and stagger off to school the next day after 10:00 A.M. Luckily, his assistant principal arrived at the high school around 6:00 A.M. and solved the morning problems. However, Jane knew that this could not go on indefinitely.

Chuck was not unhappy with the situation. For the first time in ten years, Merriam had a winning football team, and Chuck gave Jack all the credit for this. Jack was very familiar with the football surveillance tapes that were made to scout opposing teams. He had used them in Bozeman and was using them now to help the team learn unusual but effective plays. During their trips into Larabee, Jack and Chuck would go over the games time and time again. They would head into the Larabee Bar and Grill and continue their discussions over beer and pizza and not notice the time passing. Jack would forget the time in the flush of talking about victory and his favorite game—until that February night.

One February Night

It was 1:32 A.M. when Jane awoke from a sound sleep by the jolt of the telephone ringing. "Hello, who is this?" She groggily whispered into the receiver. "I'm sorry Mrs. Armstrong, this is Sheriff Meade. Your husband and Chuck Forester were driving from Larabee tonight and their car swerved and hit a fifty-two-year-old man, killing him. I'm sorry to tell you, but your husband was driving with a .25 alcohol level. This is a sad day for Merriam, Mrs. Armstrong, a sad day for the victim, and a very sad day for Jack."

Was there any way this incident could have been avoided?

Machiavelli

The people will admire those who accomplish great deeds, such as winning at important games in the territory. These games are important to the populace because they validate the worth of the community in the eyes of many. They cannot be underestimated.

However important these games may be, it is also important to gauge the sense of the populace. Do they attend the church more than the tavern? Are they soon to forgive or do they hold strong grudges for many years?

It seems in this case that the principal became wrapped up in the life of games and did not lead an exemplary life. The life of a leader is held up as a beacon to the populace. They must see the leader as beyond reproach even though the leader may be accomplishing evil at times underneath this veneer of good. The fatal flaw in Jack's case was being caught in actions that were not exemplary to the populace. This, a good prince must not do.

Lincoln

I feel that a solid relationship with the family is to be treasured above all. I cannot emphasize enough that during the dark days of the war, it was a great comfort to tell of my woes to my wife Mary. She would listen to me as best she could, but even more, she would just be there for me during the bad times.

I understand the friendship that formed between Jack and Chuck. They both served the populace under similar pressure. I had a similar pressure once. When I was in business with my late partner, we both took on much debt. When he died and left me with the total debt, I worked very hard over several years to repay the balance. This effort gained me much friendship.

Early on in his employment, Jack should have visited with his superintendent and discussed the pressures of the job and set limits on how much time he could dedicate to the football team. In this way, he could have set limits and still fulfilled his responsibilities.

STUDY QUESTIONS

(*1*) What kinds of legal repercussions will Jack Armstrong probably face?

(*2*) What does the description of the community tell you about how they will respond to Jack's actions?

(*3*) Should Jack have taken the job in the first place knowing the demands of the community and the job?

(*4*) What role should Jack's wife have played in this scenario? Could she have acted any differently to have avoided this crisis?

(*5*) Is there any way a high school principal can avoid spending the majority of his or her nights at the school?

(*6*) Was Jack correct in appointing his assistant principal to the task of early morning supervision?

(*7*) Do you think that the community will have any sympathy for Jack's misfortune?

SUGGESTED READINGS

Alexander, K. and Alexander, D. (1992). *American public school law.* Third edition. St. Paul, MN: West Publishing Co.

Shoop, R. J. (1992). *School law for the principal.* Needham Heights, MA: Allyn & Bacon Publishing.

CHAPTER 11

School Safety and Tort Liability

SAFETY is a critical issue in the schools of America. This is true regardless of the size, location, and makeup of the community from which the student population is drawn. Keeping schools safe for students is a major responsibility of any school principal and involves school law, the correlates of the effective-schools research, and the duty to protect.

Depending upon the circumstances, principals may be held responsible when students in their care are hurt or injured. When such an injury occurs a tort may arise.

The word *tort* is derived from the Latin word "to twist" or "to cause a harm." In modern day legal terms, a tort is a civil wrong and not a contractual violation. Contractual violations occur when one party of a mutual contract violates the terms of the agreement. Torts, by contrast, have several elements that are not ensconced in contractual violations.

(*1*) There is an element of negligence involving some breach of duty to protect another person from harm.

(*2*) An affirmative duty to protect must be present. In the case of school children, this duty is assumed by the school principal or teacher whenever the children participate in some type of school program that is controlled largely by the school.

(*3*) When the child is enrolled in the school and placed under the care of the school (teacher, principal, or other employee), a standard of care is presumed to exist. That standard of care must meet the reasonableness test in order to be proper.

(*4*) Torts exist only if an injury results in an actual loss (physical harm, permanent injury) in combination with a legal connection to the injury or loss.

(*5*) In schools, commonly held duties and appropriate standards of care

59

Relevant Skill

7. Awareness of the state code

---

in connection with supervision, instruction, maintenance, administration, and punishment are all areas that affect torts.

(6) Policymakers (board members) often enjoy immunity from torts when their actions are purely discretionary versus ministerial in nature. Many states have imposed limits on amounts that may be claimed in legal actions or severely restricted the areas that may be used for (risk exposure). For example, Texas permits torts only when school vehicles are involved, and Oregon limits the amounts that may be awarded to individuals in tort claims.

(7) In cases where a student's civil liberties are involved, violations may have occurred frequently in the past. However, most issues of "tort liability" revolve around the elements of failure to protect, negligence, casual connection, and standard of care.

In many states, the doctrine of governmental immunity, "the king can do no wrong," has been modified by state legislatures and the courts as it pertains to recovery of damages for actions committed by school administrators, school boards, and other employees of schools. The prospective school administrator needs to research the situation on a state-by-state basis.

SCHOOL SAFETY: MIRRORS ON AMERICAN SOCIETY

The Highland School District is a district in transition within an area that has changed over the last decade. The district population of over 50,000 was more than 100,000 a few short years ago. The well-tended homes that once belonged to the skilled workers from the area's industry are empty and falling down. Many homes have windows with broken glass and cracked panes, like wounded cyclops. Highland High School, the area's local high school, was once well-tended and maintained, garnering many honors in sports and academics. However, recently the school had fallen on difficult times because of budget cuts. The years of neglect had taken their toll in broken tiles in the laboratories, poor night lighting, and lots of graffiti. The result of the changing demographics was a middle-class exodus from the Highland area and an increasing number of minorities of mixed ethnic background. The budget cuts reduced the manpower hours for security at a time when many student discipline problems were beginning to erupt. The sale and distribution of drugs and related gang violence was a typical daily occurrence; overt selling of drugs occurs at the local hamburger stand across the street from the school. Though the problems were widely reported in the press, conservative elements in the district and on the school board continued to push for heavier reductions in the budget.

Marcia Garza and her parents had recently moved to the Highland High School District where her father worked as a security guard at a local manufacturing plant. Marcia enrolled as a sophomore at Highland Senior High School where she was immediately popular. She became involved in cheerleading, band, Spanish club and Tri-High sorority and quickly developed into an outstanding student.

Late one winter afternoon when Marcia entered the girls' restroom, she was assaulted. The restroom was located in an isolated area of the campus bounded by overgrown shrubs and was poorly lighted. Her assailant, a special education student who had been diagnosed as "emotionally disabled," was known to be violent towards others, especially women, to use drugs, and to be involved in gang-related activities. However, the district's policy on inclusion required that he be mainstreamed into the regular school program. The students' individualized educational plan was silent on the issue of discipline.

During an investigation, it was discovered that there had been a number of incidents in the past in the restroom area and that the location had been patrolled by district security personnel. However, because of budget problems, higher-level administration had cut back security two days prior to this incident.

How should this matter be handled?

Machiavelli

Choosing a minister (counselor) is a matter of no small importance. Counselors will be good or bad, depending upon the judgement rendered. The true measure of a leader's intelligence is the manner in which those who surround the leader are selected. When the counselors are able, loyal, and true to the prince, then the prince is also wise. To be sure, the leader is wise enough to select those who are able and to command their loyalty. When the ministers are otherwise, a poor opinion of the leader may be formed owing to the fact that an error was made the very first time.

Select an experienced legal counselor to work your way through the legal quagmire. It is important to avoid any blame in this matter. Deflect the criticism to the operations manager of plant and facilities. In this way the board of directors will avoid public criticism of its policies. Conversely, you may plant the seeds of discontent on those who promoted the policies that led to the debacle. In this manner you discredit them and regain your power and status.

Lincoln

All leaders require accurate and up-to-date information. While the incident described is unfortunate and should not have happened, it should be used to prevent future occurrences. Treat the offended party fairly. In this way, you will soften the mistreatment suffered. Negotiate a fair settlement, as the incident is not the fault of the affected party.

Revisit the policy of cutbacks in the area of student safety. Be forceful in demanding reinstatement of security measures. This may involve having the attorney for the board speak to it about the consequences of tort liability. Do not act out of haste or vindictiveness, as this will gain you nothing. Do not avoid the issues of responsibility; accept blame where blame is due.

Send trusted advisors to gather the necessary information regarding all aspects of the case. Only in this manner can informed decisions be made.

STUDY QUESTIONS

(*1*) How does the new move for full inclusion impact the reality of managing a complex organization such as a school? Does full inclusion fit in all situations? Is the concept of full inclusion based upon research or monetary concerns?

(*2*) Can you identify the policy issues involved in the scenario above? What are they?

(*3*) Discuss the ramifications of the policies proposed in this scenario.

(*4*) As a school site leader, how would you cope with the cutbacks in school safety? Would school safety under the conditions described in the scenario be worth laying your job on the line for? Are there other alternatives?

(*5*) Do you agree or disagree with the advice from Machiavelli? If so, what aspects do you agree with or what don't you agree with and why?

(*6*) Can you make an assessment as to the outcome of the scenario based upon what you now know of school law? How does the concept of tort liability fit into the above scenario?

(*7*) Based upon your current understanding of tort liability, who would you suggest is going to be held responsible legally for the incident described above? Why? Can you provide a defense for any or all of the respondents in the case?

(*8*) What could have been the role of the legal advisor to the district based upon what has been portrayed above?

SUGGESTED READINGS

Alexander, K. and Alexander, D. (1992). *American public school law.* Third edition. St. Paul, MN: West Publishing Co.

Data Research Inc. (1994). *Desktop encyclopedia of American school law.* Rosemont, MN: Author.

Fischer, L., Schimmel, D. and Kelly, C. (1994). *Teachers and the law.* Fourth edition. White Plains, NY: Longman Publishing Inc.

Rothstein, L. (1995). *Special education law.* Second edition. White Plains, NY: Longman Publishing Inc.

Tucker, B. (1994). *Federal disability law.* Nutshell Series. St. Paul, MN: West Publishing Co.

CHAPTER 12

Instructional Standards

WHILE much has been written about Total Quality Management (TQM), as first popularized by Dr. W. Edwards Deming, it is difficult to find information on the application of TQM to the schools. TQM as put forth by Dr. Deming involves using statistical analysis to pinpoint problems within an organization before the problem becomes visible to the consumer.

In education, this can have several meanings and applications of direct importance to the building-level administrator. TQM and statistical process-control techniques may be used in everything from tracking discipline on school grounds to tracking weaknesses in curriculums used in the school.

Even though much has been written about ''authentic assessment'' or ''portfolio assessment,'' the use and the abuse of standardized tests are still very much with us. These tests will in all probability not go away any time soon. As a result, learning how to use basic statistics in maintaining a quality school curriculum is of vital importance to the aspiring administrator.

IS IMPROVEMENT ALWAYS IMPROVEMENT?

The Southside School District was rapidly changing because of a variety of factors. Southside was located in an area of the state that was blessed with exceptional weather, scenery, recreational potential, and a work force that still had the work ethic of prewar America. The population had expanded several times, resulting in overcrowded conditions within the schools. While test scores had never been terrible by any definition, the tests were reflective of the lower-middle-class standards of the community. For years, the district had utilized the Stanford

---

Relevant Skills

1. Knowing how to evaluate staff
3. Knowing how to design a data-based improvement process
7. Awareness of the state code
11. Knowing how to relate to school board members
19. Portraying self-confidence on the job
20. Having a vision along with the knowledge of how to achieve it

---

Achievement tests as the basis for the district testing program. Recently, testing had become an issue in the district owing to increasing parental activism.

Additionally, as new patrons moved into the district demanding and expecting more from the school, conflict erupted. Most recently, two long-time members of the board of directors had been defeated at the polls. The new members of the board of directors were executives from some of the newer companies that had relocated into Southside.

At the monthly meeting of the board of directors, the superintendent announced a new policy that "required" all teachers to submit lesson plans written in behavioral terms. The superintendent solemnly announced that the public had lost its confidence in the ability of the district and that erosion of confidence had to cease.

The superintendent stressed that teacher evaluations could not continue as they had in the past, that is, confined to the way content was taught rather than focusing on outcomes. While teacher objectives had been stated in general terms, there was a need to improve student test scores. "What the public is demanding is results. The teachers are tired and set in their ways, so they will have to be pushed hard to move them to the new policy." The new school board members nodded silently in agreement, and the other members of the board sat quietly.

A teacher representative sitting in the audience could take no more. The representative glared at the superintendent and proceeded to respond to the superintendent's remarks. "How do the members of the board know how we are performing?" he asked. "We have seen no data to indicate where we stand in relation to other districts or even to our own internally defined curriculum. What happens to the district's adopted curriculum is anyone's guess once it hits the classroom," the representative stated. "We have just recently initiated site-based management, and yet we were not consulted on this very important issue. Maybe if blame is to be cast, it should be placed at the door of the central administration."

Mr. Plessy, the elementary principal, had been sitting quietly in the corner; his stomach turned over and over. Later in his office, Mr. Plessy pondered his options. He knew in talking to several of his most trusted teachers that there was much resentment over the new policy. Some of the teachers did not comply with the new policy, while others (mostly the new teachers) turned in behavioral objectives that were remarkably well done. Some teachers turned in what amounted to as a clutter of disassociated words having little to do with the new policy.

As he pondered his next move, Mr. Plessy reflected back on what he had learned in his curriculum classes about curriculum alignment.

Putting yourself in the place of Mr. Plessy, what approach to curriculum alignment would you take? Is an aligned curriculum appropriate?

Machiavelli

Ignore the dictates of the board of directors. No one from the central office reviews the lesson plans of the teachers, and what the teacher does inside the confines of the classroom is difficult to assess anyway. If asked to submit samples, delay until the policy can be changed. In the meantime, continue to build relationships with the staff members in your building.

Lincoln

Above all, be ethical in your reaction to the new policy. Make an appointment with the assistant superintendent of instruction to clarify what the new policy means. How is the new policy going to be implemented? What are going to be the guidelines for monitoring the behavioral objectives? In the meantime, make plans for staff development on the issue.

STUDY QUESTIONS

(*1*) Assume that you are Mr. Plessy, what would your course of action be?

(2) Assuming that you are hired as an outside consultant, what would you propose to salvage the situation?

(3) What impact might the newly elected board members have upon the superintendent's actions? How might Mr. Plessy modify the new directives at his school site?

(4) What does the available research say on test scores as indicators of school success?

(5) How do the effective-school correlates fit into this scenario?

(6) What happens when the measure of a school's effectiveness is reduced to test scores?

(7) Many elements in American society are convinced that America's decline as an economic power is directly related to the decline in test scores. What would your response to that assumption be and what might you base your response on?

(8) Assume that your board of education mandates that all teachers must write lesson plans in behavioral terms. How would you as a building administrator implement the policy? Would the proposed policy be worth laying your job on the line for?

(9) What does Raymond Callahan have to say about how American education evolved from the business model, and how does this scenario fit into his historical overview?

(10) What does the literature say about the semiprofessionals?

SUGGESTED READINGS

Airasian, P. W. (1985). *The ninth mental measurements yearbook, Volume I.* Buros Institute of mental measurements. University of Nebraska, Lincoln, NE. Iowa Tests of Basic Skills, Forms 7 and 8, Boston College, Chestnut Hill, MA.

A report—The governor's task force on effective schooling. (1981). Alaska State Department of Education, Administrative Order #64.

Barrett, S. Unpublished film slides. Springfield School District No. 19. 525 Mill Street, Springfield, OR 97477.

Bonstingel, J. (1992). *Schools of quality: An introduction to total quality management in education.* Alexandria, VA: Association for Supervision and Curriculum Development.

Cairns, Donald V. (1990). Differences in organizational structure between selected elementary and secondary school in Washington State, Doctoral Dissertation Washington State University, 1990. *Dissertation Abstracts International.*

Caplan, M. K. and O'Rourke, T. J. (1988). Improving student achievement on standardized tests: One approach. *NASSP Bulletin,* 72(505):54−58.

Cooperman, S. and Bloom, J. (1985). *Getting the most from the New Jersey HSPT: A practical guide to resolving curriculum design and delivery problems.* Farmington, MA: Center for Teaching and Learning Mathematics (ERIC Document Reproduction Service No. ED 278-713).

Crowell, R. (1986). *Curriculum alignment.* Washington, DC: Office of Research and Improvement (ERIC Document Reproduction Service No. ED 280-874).

Curriculum alignment with the essential learning skills. (1985). Unpublished materials, Oregon State Department of Education, 700 Pringle Parkway SE, Salem, OR 97310-0290.

English, F. (1987). *Curriculum management for schools, colleges and business.* Springfield, IL: Charles C. Thomas Publishing.

Firestone, W. A. and Herriott, R. E. (1982). Prescriptions for effective elementary schools don't fit secondary schools. *Educational Leadership,* 40(3):51−53.

Fortune, J. C. and Cromack, T. R. (1987). *Test Critiques, Volume III.* Test Corporation of America. Metropolitan achievement test: 5th edition. Blacksburg, VA: Polytechnic Institute and State University.

Fry, E. (1980). Test review: Metropolitan achievement tests. *The Reading Teacher.* New Brunswick, NJ: Rutgers University.

Getzels, J. W. (1958). Administration as a social process. In Halprin, A. (ed.). *Administrative Theory in Education.* Chicago, IL: Midwest Administrative Center, pp. 140−165.

Hall, G. and Hord, S. (1987). *Change in schools: Facilitating the process.* Albany, NY: State University of New York Press.

Hanson, M. E. (1985). *Educational administrative and organizational behavior.* Allyn & Bacon Publishing, pp. 36, 297.

Hathaway, W. et al. (1985). A regional and local item response theory based on a test item bank system. Portland Public Schools, Department of Research and Evaluation (ERIC Document Reproduction Service No. ED 284-883).

Henson, K. T. and Saterfiel, T. H. (1985). State mandated accountability programs: Are they educationally sound? *NASSP Bulletin,* 69(477):23−27.

Hersey, P. and Blanchard, K. (1977). *Management of organizational behavior: Utilizing human resources.* Second edition. Englewood Cliffs, NJ: Prentice-Hall.

Hersey, P. and Blanchard, K. (1982). *Management of organizational behavior: Utilizing human resources.* Third edition. Englewood Cliffs, NJ: Prentice-Hall.

Hersey, P. and Blanchard, K. (1988). *Management of organizational behavior: Utilizing human resources.* Fourth edition. Englewood Cliffs, NJ: Prentice-Hall.

Hersey, P. and Blanchard, K. (1993). *Management of organizational behavior: Utilizing human resources.* Sixth edition. Englewood Cliffs, NJ: Prentice-Hall.

Hertel, E. H. (1978). *Metropolitan achievement tests.* Fifth edition. *The Ninth Mental Measurements Yearbook,* pp. 959−968.

Lezotte, L. W. and Bancroft, B. A. (1986). School improvement based upon effective schools research. *Outcomes, a Quarterly Journal of the Network for Outcome Based Schools,* 6(1):13−17.

Liberman, A. and Miller, L., eds. (1984). *Teachers, their world, and their work: Implications for school.* Alexandria, VA: Association for Supervision and Curriculum Development.

Lortie, D. (1975). *School teacher.* Chicago, IL: University of Chicago Press, chapter 8.

Mann, D. (1986). Testimony given is support of H. B. 747. *Outcomes,* 6(1):10.

Mehrens, W. A. (1984). National tests and local curriculum: Match or mismatch? *Educational Measurement: Issues and Practices,* Fall:9−15.

Miller, S. L., Cohen, S. R. and Sayre, K. A. (1985). Significant achievement gains using the effective school model. *Educational Leadership,* March:38−43.

Nidermeyer, F. and Yelon, S. (1981). Los Angeles aligns instruction with essential learning skills. *Educational Leadership,* May:618−620.

Spady, G. W. and Marx, G. (1984). *Excellence in our schools: Making it happen.* American Association of School Administrators and Far West Laboratory, 1801 North Moore Street, Arlington, VA 22209.

Walton, M. (1986). *The Deming management method.* New York, NY: Perigree Books.

Weick, K. E. (1976). Educational organizations as loosely coupled systems. *Administrative Science Quarterly,* 21:1−19.

Weick, K. (1979). *The social psychology of organizing.* Second edition. Reading, MA: Addison-Wesley Publishing Company.

Weick, K. E. (1982). Administering education in loosely coupled systems. *Phi Delta Kappan,* 63(10):673−676.

CHAPTER 13

Job Dissatisfaction

EVEN though one might have all the technical answers, as well as a workable leadership style, fate sometimes lends a cruel blow to the best laid plans. The following case presents an incident that was not anticipated, even by those who understand finances. This involves the support team at the school, and concerns those who support its instructional vision. The management and evaluation of food-service workers, custodians, and secretarial staff is important in this scenario.

THE LAYOFF

Wednesday Morning 8:00 A.M.

The atmosphere at Dunsmuir High School seemed as gray as the clouds on the December morning that the custodial staff gathered in the small maintenance room.

John Bacon, head of the custodial staff read the headlines: "Staff Layoffs at Dunsmuir High School."

Additional articles on the front page told the sad story of a major $2 billion county treasurer error. John was unable to understand the entire story. But evidently the treasurer had been borrowing to invest in risky notes to achieve a higher rate of return, or something like that. Anyway, he felt that the classified staff would feel the brunt of the cutbacks — as usual.

"It says here that the food services, custodial and secretarial staff will suffer the greatest percentage of cutbacks. Well! Isn't that always the case? And would you believe this? They are trying to forget about seniority and want to maintain staff based on merit! What the heck does that mean? I can't believe it!"

Relevant Skills

1. Knowing how to evaluate staff
8. Knowing how to manage operational services
9. Establishing a positive relationship with other administrators
13. Understanding how the principalship changes one's family relationships
18. Knowing why one was selected for leadership
19. Portraying self-confidence on the job
21. Desiring to make a difference in the lives of staff and students
23. Understanding that change is ongoing
24. Knowing how to assess job responsibilities

The two other custodians muttered their agreement. What was going on? You would think that the principal, Mr. Osborne, would not keep them in the dark like a bunch of mushrooms!

John continued, ''What a shot right before Christmas! And all because of a treasurer's mistake. It's time to contact our union representative and think about lawsuits!'' The other two chimed in their agreement.

That Same Morning: Mr. Osborne, in the Principal's Office, Talking to Mrs. Sanders, the Vice Principal

''Mary, I can't believe that this is happening. The superintendent is telling me that I have to cut $200,000 from this budget. You know I can't do it without touching the classified staff. I can't cut teachers. In addition, the unions are going to be suing us because of contract violations. The superintendent is saying not to worry about seniority! I can't believe it! It seems that if there are legitimately no funds, then they have the right to ignore seniority!'' Tom Osborne paused. ''All this job dissatisfaction caused by an error in the treasurer's office. This is something over which we have no control! The morale in this place is nonexistent! Even the teaching staff is feeling the heat!''

''Tom, I know you take this seriously,'' said Mary, ''but you can't take it personally. I'll see you after the lunch break, and we can talk about this more. We'll have to change the custodial schedule, serve the lunches ourselves, and have the teachers clean their own rooms. But, we'll survive—we'll survive. Of course, we'll have to rely on temporary workers if we want to get the lawn cut. I'm not that clever with a lawn mower." Mary slipped out to attend to the recess.

Tom reflected back on his two years as the principal of Dunsmuir High. When he first arrived, he found the staff split on loyalty—a common occurrence when the new person arrives after the previous principal had served for ten years. He didn't try to duplicate a previous style, but brought in his own expertise. He felt he had finally brought the whole teaching and support staff together—and now this!

He looked at a copy of the school budget before him. Maybe there was a way to make cuts away from the classroom that would not eliminate his entire support staff. But as he studied the figures for the tenth time, he began to see that this idea was hopeless. How could he cut a computer lab that was just installed this year? How could he try to increase already overcrowded classes?

He took out a stack of evaluations of his support staff over the last three years. Where to begin? Where to begin?

What will be the result of Tom's elimination of most of his full time custodial, food services and secretarial staff? Are there any other options that Tom might explore that he cannot see now?

Machiavelli

Auxiliary armies are useless in the field. They are no better than mercenaries in their loyalty to you and to their job. Even though your full-time troops may support you, as in this case, in times of chaos and misfortune, even they will turn on you. And you cannot foresee every misfortune that is within your time.

There may be more options than this prince can see at this time. Perhaps a neighboring high school can share forces. This may be an opportunity to gain strength from neighbors and cement relationships for years to come. Neighbors come to help even for nefarious reasons, which you may find out only later.

It is important that the prince keep at least one loyal minister in each of his support forces. This full-time minister will help to form the nucleus of the remaining troops. A prince must always anticipate the future.

Lincoln

It appears that this general did what all good generals do—he walked the fields with his support troops and gained their loyalty when he first assumed his employment. This has served him in good stead even in these tough times.

My secretaries have mentioned to me that sometimes I spend 75 percent of my time out of my office, on my terms. I would even break into my Cabinet officers' meetings to apprise them of some important news. I met with my Cabinet at least twice a week. I met with others all the time and even interrupted affairs of the state to meet an old farmer from the Midwest.

But I knew I could not do it all. I relied on my generals in the field and even to my chagrin, stuck with them in times of misfortune. For misfortune comes to every man and to every endeavor. It must be expected. I would recommend to this general that he keep at least two good officers in every support team to keep him informed and prepare for a later rebuilding of the troops.

STUDY QUESTIONS

(1) What other scenario in a school district might be beyond a principal's "control"?

(2) Is there any strategy Tom might use to make the cuts less painful to the classified staff?

(3) Can he contract any services? What are the parameters in your district about privatization of services?

(4) Are there other options that Tom has not explored?

SUGGESTED READING

Phillips, D. T. (1992). *Lincoln on leadership*. New York, NY: Time Warner Books.

CHAPTER 14

Community Structure/ Organizational Behavior

IT is naive to believe that a community's political complexity and its ethos do not impact the position of the principal. Open systems theory tells us that schools act and react to events as they occur within the entire community and each community has its own identity, personality, and communications network. Understanding, deciphering, and assuaging all the competing forces that exist in a community are part of the school leader's job. How this job is done is crucial to meeting the school's mission and to the success of the school principal. In order to meet all the competing demands, the school principal must understand how his or her leadership style interacts with the community and the meaning of open systems theory.

Traditional bureaucratic theory teaches us that conflict is an aberration due to a failure somewhere in the management of an organizational system. Either planning was poor or there was a breakdown in the command and control structure by management. Human relations theory, on the other hand, states that conflict develops within the school because of management failure to establish norms of behavior, expectations, or group cohesion. Therefore, happy workers are productive workers in an organization that is dominated by social system beliefs. The traditionally run organization eliminates conflict by domination and exertion of some form of power. Power in traditional leadership also teaches us that the leader of the organization exerts direct leadership through the use of either a selling or telling mode.

More recently, however, school administrators have learned that working with the board of directors involves a much more detailed investigation of school board topologies. Those topologies are not always clear on the surface. A failure to properly diagnose the board topologies and not being able to conceptualize what open systems theory teaches us about school can lead to disaster.

Relevant Skills

2. Knowing how to facilitate group meetings
14. Developing interpersonal networking skills
15. Knowing how to encourage involvement by all parties
19. Portraying self-confidence on the job
23. Understanding that change is ongoing

Open systems theory postulates that conflict is inevitable and can lead to positive outcomes when creative solutions are utilized. The creative solutions and the development of these solutions are the responsibility of the principal. Whether the principal utilizes direct or indirect leadership and understands open systems theory will play a major role in how rapidly the principal moves through the stages of professional development.

IS THIS WHAT IS KNOWN AS "INPUT"?

The Futura School District was once one of the wealthiest districts within the southwestern region of the state. Futura was the center of mining and smelting for the entire state. The mines provided many jobs and economic security for what was a blue-collar workforce as well as property tax revenues that allowed the district to develop solid academic programs. Test scores were high and most graduates entered into postsecondary training programs. It was widely accepted that the Futura School District, while not highly innovative, was providing a solid educational foundation for the children of the district. Teacher salaries were among the highest in the southwest region, facilities were good, and the benefits were exceptional.

However, within recent years, the mines had closed, workers were displaced, the tax base vaporized, and the community demographics were gradually changing. Professionals moved on to more secure economic futures, young people left for better jobs, and in general, a slow economic downturn took hold. Futura, however, remained a bastion of labor. In addition, owing to the past history of mining, the city had a flavor unique for the state. Italians, Croats, Serbs, Welch, French, English, and Germans all lived and worked in the mines. This resulted in the evolution of neighborhoods that reflected the ethnic diversity. In many respects, Futura had the flavor of the larger, more settled cities of the east. Education, and in particular obtaining a job in teaching, was seen as one of the first steps to climbing out of the mines and into middle-class status. As a consequence, teaching jobs went to native sons and daughters of Futura, regardless of the specific skills that those sons and daughters brought to the district.

For years, the district board of directors had been dominated by leaders from the business district. The ethnic diversity in the community was displayed in the makeup of the school board. The Futura board of directors was composed of seven members elected by district. Of the seven board members, five were men, two were women, and ethnic diversity was reflected in the board's composition. The board of directors were elected by voters in the entire district, yet functioned on the old "ward" system prevalent in larger eastern cities. Each board member responded to the patrons of the neighborhood they lived closest to.

It was Bob Roberts's first year as principal of Futura High School. He had recently graduated from one of the state's more prestigious universities with a master's degree in school administration. Bob Roberts has an interesting background. He is the son of a very successful attorney and comes from one of the wealthiest sections of the state's southern region. His pastimes include listening to classical music, reading, stamp collecting, collecting Victorian art glass, and haunting museums. Privately, he admitted that he felt that the decline in American education was due to the fact that too much effort was spent on programs that detracted from the basic skills necessary to advance into postsecondary training.

After two months on the job and after reviewing the board's hiring policies, he obtained permission to advertise for teaching positions in the areas of science, music, literature, and mathematics. Several of the applicants were from Futura, but the best candidates were from out of the region. Bob felt that all things aside, new ideas would be good for the staff and the students in his school. While all candidates were qualified for the state certificate, there was a great deal of difference in quality between the applications.

Acting upon the district policies for hiring, Bob made his recommendations to the board with the full knowledge of the central office. Each of his recommendations was for the hiring of "outsiders." All of the native candidates, while theoretically in the pool, were far down his list. In fact, none of the natives were in the top ten.

The reaction was immediate. ''If we can't have a say in things, then why sit on the board of directors?'' responded the board chairman.

''I agree,'' stated the vice chairman of the board.

''I move that we hire Joe Nesbitt; I have known his family for years and they are all good people,'' stated one of the male board members.

The board chair called for a vote, and Joe Nesbitt was hired unanimously. Bob was stunned! Nesbitt was his last choice among all of the candidates and had mediocre recommendations to say the least. He hadn't even been interviewed by his building personnel review team! What to do now!

Machiavelli

Ruling often results from gaining power from the people or from the barons, depending upon which has a chance to prevail. When the barons see that the power stems from that of the people, they will promote one of their own so that they may act in his/her shadow. Likewise, when the people see that power of the barons has grown, they build up one of their kind so as to gain authority in order to have a protective shield. One who gains power with the aid of the nobility has more difficulty in retaining the position. One cannot keep the nobility satisfied over the long term, as the barons believe themselves to be the leader's equal, and they are unable to take orders from a peer. However, one can satisfy the commoners as their goals are more honest than those of the nobility. The common people want only to be left alone. Either the barons manage their affairs so as to follow your lead or they desire to lead you. When they indicate that they desire to lead, they then are thinking more about themselves and their fortunes than about those of the people or the kingdom.

Build up your alliances with the common people for that is where the strength lies. Lay the ground work for the failure of the new hire so as to embarrass the nobles by this appointment. In that way, you may be able to change the policy directly.

Lincoln

Loyalty is often won over by private conversation so that the other fellow may understand your point of view. Every effective leader must understand that the ability to lead is predicated upon the ability to communicate effectively. In most businesses, private conversation is more important than public speaking. A failure to "grease the wheel" causes the squeak to gain the upper hand. When policies are blindly followed, disaster is in the making.

Accept your new hire and strive to make the most of the person's abilities. To do otherwise is as immoral as it is dangerous. Resolve to communicate the processes more adequately in the future, and try in all cases to hire the most adequate local personages that are available. Rely on outside applicants only after exhausting all other avenues. In either case, be prepared to offer the best local candidate or forego the recommendation of any candidate.

STUDY QUESTIONS

(*1*) How did Bob contribute to his own problems?

(*2*) Would you try to assist the new hire out the door or help that person to become all that he or she could become? Why?

(*3*) What is the danger of either course of action?

(*4*) How did the community makeup contribute to the decision?

(*5*) Even in much larger systems, can the local parents impact the hiring process in negative or unwanted ways? How? If not, then how?

(*6*) What does the local policy in your current district say? What has been the trend in your district?

(*7*) What might be the long-term consequences of policies that favor the hiring of locals? Are there positive aspects to consider?

(*8*) What does the literature say about the hiring processes? Is the literature too "academic" or too "pragmatic?"

(*9*) What is your belief about the proper balance in the hiring process? Is hiring a "precise" science?

(*10*) Assuming that you are in command of a school, how are you going to hire? What are your procedures going to be and what might you do to forestall disaster?

SUGGESTED READINGS

Bailey, F. G. (1965). Decisions by consensus in councils and committees: With specific reference to village and local government of India. In M. Banton (ed.). *Political system and the distribution of power.* Columbus, OH: Frederich A. Prager Publishers, pp. 1–20.

Barge, Kevin J. (1994). *Leadership: Communication skills for organizations and groups.* New York, NY: St. Martin's Press.

Brouge, Grady E. (1985). *The enemies of leadership: Lessons for leaders in education.* Bloomington, IN: Phi Delta Kappa.

Corbett, Dickson, H. (1991). Community influence and school micro-politics. In Blase, J. (ed.). *The politics of life in schools: Power, conflict and cooperation.* Newbury Park, CT: Sage Publications.

Hanson, Mark. (1991). *Educational administration and organizational behavior.* Third edition. Needham Heights, MA: Allyn & Bacon Publishing, pp. 142–148.

Owens, Robert G. (1995). *Organizational behavior in education.* Fifth edition. Needham Heights, MA: Allyn & Bacon Publishing, pp. 146–165.

Rada, R. (1984). Community dissatisfaction and school governance. *Planning and Changing,* 15(4):234–247.

Rada, R. (1989). A political context framework for the study of local school governance. Unpublished manuscript.

Vidich, A. and Bensman, J. (1968). *Small town in mass society: Class, power, and religion in a rural community.* Princeton, NJ: Princeton University Press.

Webb, Dean et al. (1987). *Personnel administration in education.* Columbus, OH: Merrily Publishing Company, pp. 77–91.

Wirt, F. and Kirst, M. (1972). *The political web of American schools.* Boston, MA: Little, Brown and Co.

Wirt, F. and Kirst, M. (1982). *The politics of education: Schools in conflict.* Berkeley, CA: McCutchan Publishing Corporation.

Zeigler, H. and Jennings, M. with Peak, W. (1974). *Governing American schools: Political interaction in local school districts.* North Sciuate, MA: Duxbury Press.

CHAPTER 15

Effective Schools and Parental Expectations

IN the recent headlong rush to create school-site councils, generate outcome-based education, and meet increased state and federal mandates, the research on effective schools has largely been overlooked. However, that research is as valuable today as when it was first published in the 1970s and early 1980s. The work of Brookhover (1981), Brookhover et al. (1973, 1977), Brookhover and Lezotte (1979), Lezotte (1984), Firestone and Herriott (1981), Firestone and Wilson (1984), Deal (1985), and others still offers many insights into how to create an effective public school.

A distillation of the effective-school correlates states that in order to be defined as effective, a school should have the following characteristics (Cairns, 1990):

(1) Clearly defined goals
(2) Regular evaluations of program and staff
(3) Rules that are designed to assist the organization in meeting its clearly defined goals
(4) High expectations for staff and students

While there are other correlates that may be included in the list, the common core of what the effective-schools research states is intact. However, creating an effective school and listing the correlates of an effective school are often easier to do in the abstract than in reality.

Creating a more effective school requires the school principal to have detailed knowledge of the school culture, to understand his or her leadership style, and to have the technical skills necessary to generate such a school. When what is known about leadership theory, organizational behavior, and change processes is utilized, a valuable set of tools

---

Relevant Skills

1. Knowing how to evaluate staff
2. Knowing how to facilitate group meetings
3. Knowing how to design a data-based improvement process
5. Knowing how to conduct parent-student-teacher conferences
14. Developing interpersonal networking skills
16. Maintaining positive relationships with other agencies
20. Having a vision along with the knowledge of how to achieve it

---

becomes available to the school administrator who wants to generate an effective school.

However, it is all too easy to forget these lessons when one is immersed in the day-to-day operations of a school and dealing with real human crises. It is important that the beginning administrator remember that there is a linkage between the theory and the practice of school administration. It just does not always seem so. During the change process, it is very easy to make a mess of things when all that is desired is to create a more effective school.

YOU WANT TO DO WHAT?

Mary had come to Apple Valley after serving two years as an elementary principal in another part of the state. In her last district, she was known as an innovator, one of the up and coming new administrators, having recently completed her master's degree in educational leadership.

While at the local university, she had become interested in what the literature had to say about "effective schools." She was determined to make Apple Valley Elementary into a model of the effective school's research. As a result, Mary dug into the school files in a frenzy of work, collecting data to bolster her cause. Mary's research was quite revealing, as the test scores reflected a school achieving well below what it should, given the socioeconomic standard of the attendance area. The personnel files also reflected a laissez-faire attitude toward some of the teaching staff. Many teachers had been transferred into Apple Valley as a result of disciplinary measures taken by the central office.

Apple Valley School was in a middle-class neighborhood that had many nice, well-maintained homes. Most of the families that lived and worked in Apple Valley were employed as skilled workers in a light manufacturing plant that was located nearby. However, the test scores of the school mirrored some of the poorer, inner-city schools, and left Mary confused. The test results should have been much higher and not reflective of a low-economic neighborhood. Apple Valley was reflective of middle income values and attitudes. There were many churches (predominately of evangelical background) in the area, low numbers of saloons, a healthy downtown, and a new mall that spoke of an increasing level of prosperity.

Over the weekend, Mary gave her findings much thought. Instinctively, she knew that if she walked into the school and started trying to implement the effective-schools correlates that the implication would be that Apple Valley was not a good school. Upon reflection, she decided that she would invite one of her university professors to give a series of presentations to the staff and PTA on outcome-based education as a way to introduce the effective-schools correlates into Apple Valley School.

On Monday morning, she made the arrangements with the professor and found the money to pay the honorarium from her staff development fund. She decided to publicize the presentations to the parents and staff and distributed flyers announcing the time and place of the series. Her excitement grew as she anticipated the school working toward positive student outcomes, increased staff engagement in their profession, and closer ties with the parents.

Thursday morning, her secretary announced, ''Mr. James, the school superintendent, would like to see you in his office and wanted me to let you know that it is *very* important.'' Upon arrival at the central office, she noticed that a delegation of parents was present, along with members of the local evangelical churches. She thought to herself, ''What in the world has happened? It couldn't possibly have anything to do with me.''

What did go wrong and what assumptions did Mary make that led her into the position that she found herself in on this Thursday morning?

Machiavelli

A ruler never disarms the populace of a kingdom. The reasons are simple: When the subjects are armed properly, their arms become the arms of the prince. In so arming the population, the prince's strength grows in proportion to the loyalty of the subjects. There are some exceptions to the above rule.

When a prince acquires a new kingdom, he must disarm those who would do him harm. Failure to do so generates dissension among the subjects and eventually leads to his downfall. The prince should be careful to arm only those that have assisted him in acquiring power, as they owe much of their own welfare to his continued reign.

By failing to adequately disarm those that would like to see you fail, you gave them strength to work against your kingdom. Now you must be ruthless in your pursuit of internal dissension. Bide thy time in rooting out those that are disloyal, you are still weak in power. Set aside your quest for excellence and concentrate on consolidating your power. When the time is right and you have planted the correct seeds, then you may move.

After the disloyal have been removed, begin developing staff by training them in the correlates of the effective-schools research. In this way, you may eventually establish outcome-based education in the school.

Lincoln

Now is not the time to pursue your goals. You must first establish strong ties to the community. Explain your reasons for how outcome-based education can improve the education for all children. Demonstrate this by showing the trend of the test results over the last three- to five-year period. Above all, be honest in your approach to those that oppose you. It is important that you do not try to take out your retribution on those who do not see things as you do. Instead, concentrate on forming alliances both inside and outside of the school community. Explain what the mission of the public schools is. Invite experts from other neighboring schools to speak on the issue of effective schools and outcome-based education. Remember, people fear that which they do not understand.

STUDY QUESTIONS

(1) Do you agree with the advice from Lincoln or Machiavelli?
(2) Which advice do you prefer? Why?

(*3*) Is there confusion over outcome-based education in your school? Why? What seems to be the rationale behind such opposition?

(*4*) How would you work in Apple Valley School to improve student outcomes?

(*5*) What is the difference between outcome-based education and student learning objectives or some other similar plan? Is a lot of the change in approach substantive or an "old wine in a new bottle"?

(*6*) What is it about outcome-based education that upsets so many parents?

(*7*) Are there other methods to improve the schools without the use of outcome-based education? If so, what are they?

(*8*) What does change theory have to say about generating long-lasting and permanent change?

(*9*) Is the effective-schools research suitable for implementation in organizations that are loosely coupled?

(*10*) If you were to implement the effective-schools research, what might be some of the unanticipated consequences? Would those consequences be positive or negative?

(*11*) How could you bring about change in an organization that is deemed to be loosely coupled?

SUGGESTED READINGS

Brookhover, W. B. (1981). *Effective secondary schools*. Philadelphia, PA: Research for Better Schools (ERIC Document Reproduction Service No. ED 231-088).

Brookhover, W., Gigliotti, R. J., Henderson, R. D. and Schneider, J. M. (1973). *Elementary school social environment and school achievement*. Final Report. East Lansing, MI: College of Urban Development, Michigan State University (ERIC Document Reproduction Service No. ED 086 306).

Brookhover, W. B. and Lezotte, L. W. (1979). *Changes in school characteristics coincident with changes in student achievement*. East Lansing, MI: Institute for Research on Teaching, Michigan State University. Occasional Paper No. 17.

Cairns, Donald V. (1990). Differences in organizational structure between selected rural elementary and secondary schools in Washington State. Doctoral Dissertation, Washington State University, 1990. *Dissertation Abstracts International*.

Deal, T. E. (1985). The symbolism of effective schools. *The Elementary School Journal*, 85(5):601–620.

Firestone, W. A. and Herriott, R. E. (1981). The bureaucratic elementary school: Comparing two images of elementary, jr. high and high schools. Paper presented at the annual meeting of the American Educational Research Association, Los Angeles, CA (ERIC Document Reproduction Service No. ED 203 532).

Firestone, W. A. and Wilson, B. L. (1984). What can principals do? Culture is a key to more effective instruction. *NASSP Bulletin,* 68:7 – 11.

Lezotte, L. W. (1984). School effectiveness research: A tribute to Ron Edmonds. One perspective on an effective schools research agenda. Paper presented at the annual meeting of the American Educational Research Association, New Orleans (ERIC Document Reproduction Service No. ED 253 961).

CHAPTER 16

Interpersonal Relationships

IN the original study that categorizes the types of skills as technical, socialization and self-awareness, it is interesting to note that the majority of these skills revolve around the self and knowledge of the self and of others.

Since the educational field is labor intensive, the knowledge of how to work with small groups, motivate and lead personnel, and simply work well with others is paramount. It is also notable that of the three top-rated skills, two are tied to working with staff and making a difference in the lives of students. Having a vision and an understanding of the steps to achieve goals is the top-rated skill.

The following case deals with the important relationship of a middle-school principal with her faculty. In such a close knit group as a faculty, favoritism is always a danger. This is a case with an unusual twist. It is a case that has the principal moving too far in one direction — one that she has a difficult time returning from.

THE ALL-STATE SEVENTH-GRADE GIRLS' MATH CONTEST

Saturday Morning, November 10, Kathy Brown's Home

Kathy Brown sat on her living room couch and read through the Saturday morning newspapers: ''Rockaway Middle School Girls' Math Club to Join All-State Contest!'' screamed the headline of the *Rockaway News*. Kathy knew that this was a great time for the town.

By Friday, she would know if her middle school was the top of the heap, home of the *crème de la crème* of girl math students. What a week it would be!

Relevant Skills

2. Knowing how to facilitate group meetings
9. Establishing a positive relationship with other administrators
10. Knowing how to delineate employee roles
14. Developing interpersonal networking skills
15. Knowing how to encourage involvement by all parties
20. Having a vision along with knowledge of how to achieve it

---

Kathy had been working for about a year with Joan Hathaway, the seventh-grade math teacher, to drill the girls' club on the basic skills that were included in the contest. Kathy was principal of Rockaway Middle School and had attended every all-state contest for the past five years. She knew what kind of questions were asked, and she was confident that she and Joan had drilled the girls on the right questions.

The contest was very personal for Kathy. She believed that her own math teachers had always belittled her and not given her the attention that they gave to the male students. "Boys are much better at figures!" was the statement she heard constantly. But this would be different!

Most of the twenty-member staff of Rockaway Middle School was behind Kathy. Even though the staff was evenly divided by gender, she felt that the male staff members were supportive. Even Mark Adams who taught the other seventh-grade math class expressed his support.

Kathy had always participated in conferences that supported math skills for women. She had supported the introduction of Title IX and always made sure that the female and male sports opportunities were equitable at her school. Kathy made it a point to spend a part of every faculty meeting discussing the strides that her school was making in equality for girl students. She made sure that field hockey was a major sport at the school. She made sure that awards favored female athletes because she believed that she was compensating for past injustices. Kathy pushed the papers aside and reflected on how she had overcome the barriers of her childhood to assume the role of principal.

Her father had tended to give the bulk of his support to her two younger brothers. When they brought home report cards with Bs, they were rewarded. But when she brought home A minuses, she was exhorted to do better. She was not encouraged to pursue her favorite sport, field hockey, because her mother and father regarded it as too masculine. Consequently, when her two brothers were accepted at Stanford and she was not, she blamed her parents for not encouraging her more to take hard subjects, such as calculus, organic chemistry, and biology. She reasoned that her brothers had gotten into Stanford because of their athletic skills and their science backgrounds. She had been able to enter a small teachers' college near her home, and she had resented this opportunity even when she finally graduated with honors. She ended up majoring in science and math and teaching it at a local middle school. She would show them that a woman could succeed at the hard sciences!

After teaching for five years, she acquired her administrative certificate and became assistant principal at the school. From then on, it was easy to advance to a middle school in the next county, and she became its principal two years ago.

Monday Afternoon Faculty Meeting

Kathy started the meeting, ''I know some of you have questioned my conducting an all girls' math class for the past year. Perhaps this was an unorthodox way to raise the math scores of our female students. I know you are all pleased, however, that our girl students are competing in All State this Thursday night. I know you will put our differences behind you and support our girls at the capital.'' The teachers gave knowing looks to each other, while Kathy continued.

''One thing that strikes me as interesting is that the classes with boys on this campus have not kept their scores on an even par with the girls. Now *that's* what I call progress! Everyone said it couldn't be done.''

She ended the faculty meeting with an invitation for all the faculty to join her and Joan at the contest Thursday evening.

Thursday Night at the Contest

Kathy beamed as she realized that her students would be next on the program. She was disappointed that no other members of the faculty were there to share her triumph. She looked over at Joan who was striding over to her with a worried look on her face. This wasn't like Joan to look perturbed before a contest.

''What's up Joan? Did we lose any of our girls?''

''No,'' Joan responded, ''but I think that you had better hear something from me before you hear it from someone else. You are being sued by the male teachers on your staff for unequal treatment of both male and female staff members and unequal treatment of male and female students. And here's the news that's the real topper! Both the women and men on your staff signed the original petition! The superintendent wants you to call him right now — and he made it clear it was right now!''

What had Kathy done that precipitated this problem? How could she have avoided it?

Machiavelli

There is always unequal treatment of subjects as far as the prince is concerned. There is no way that the prince can avoid this, and it is natural. I do not understand in this case, though, why the younger women are treated with more care than men. This is against nature, as women are by nature timid and should be cared for in the home. At least this was done in my time with no great harm to the municipalities.

How one treats his or her army is very important. One must have loyal troops in order to be strong. Troops know when favoritism is rampant, and they make known their dislike of this practice. It appears here that the principal was not aware of the feelings of the troops as they assumed the guise of flattery until they were sure of their goals. It is too late to bring this tale from disaster. Kathy will be removed, and a fair ruler will take her place.

Lincoln

Even though I have been a lawyer for many years, I am unfamiliar with Title IX and the legal principles that it represents. It appears to concern equal treatment under the law without regard to gender or race, so I am sure that I could defend this in court. Back in Illinois, I defended many and brought justice to many. I used stories to illustrate my points rather than lecture on issues of law.

This story reminds me of two of my wartime generals. One general treated his army with great respect. He gave equal weight to his officers — long-time or short-time friendships aside. The other officer favored a select few whom he had known before the war. You can be sure that the fairly treated officers were much more loyal to their general.

I am pained to assert that it would be best for all for Kathy to retire from the scene and take care to learn from her mistakes.

STUDY QUESTIONS

(*1*) How did her childhood affect Kathy's management style?

(*2*) How does Title IX affect this case?

(*3*) Does past treatment suggest that girls should spend more time than boys do learning math skills?

(*4*) How is the advice of Lincoln and Machiavelli similar? How is it different?

(*5*) Is a math competition a good idea for middle-school students?

(*6*) Should Kathy stay out of the operation of the competition?

SUGGESTED READING

Deal, T. and Kennedy, A. (1982). *Corporate cultures*. Reading, MA: Addison-Wesley.

Case Study Decision Analysis

MARK an X on where you stand:

	Laissez-faire	Lincoln's View	Machiavelli's View
Case Study 1			
Case Study 2			
Case Study 3			
Case Study 4			
Case Study 5			
Case Study 6			
Case Study 7			
Case Study 8			
Case Study 9			
Case Study 10			
Case Study 11			
Case Study 12			
Case Study 13			
Case Study 14			
Case Study 15			
Case Study 16			

PRINCIPAL TRAINING

EACH year thousands of new principals assume the educational leadership of a school for the first time. Typically they have taken education courses that include finance, law, and leadership. They probably have filled a vice principalship or similar job assignment before they assumed the position of principal. But nothing really prepares them for the task ahead. Many principals have complained about their training and how it does not prepare them for the job. In truth, many professors disagree about what kinds of training are right for the job the principal will confront.

WHAT THE LITERATURE TELLS US

Each new principal arrives on the job with a diverse set of skills, beliefs, and experience. He or she typically is excited and is eager to work through each issue calmly and expeditiously, without raising serious political issues. Unfortunately, the spotlight is upon that new principal—especially for the first two years. What the novice does in those crucial years may indelibly mark the success or nonsuccess of an entire career. Therefore, the well-prepared principal has the upper hand when it comes to setting up career longevity.

THE CONTENT OF THIS TEXT—ITS UTILITY AND APPLICABILITY

This text contains sixteen case studies that are designed to give the reader an overview of the types of cases that come up on a regular basis in the schools. They include situations found at elementary, middle, and high schools and involve discussions on technical, conceptual, socialization, and self-awareness issues. The cases begin with an identification of the precise skills that are used in the study. Opinions of Lincoln and Machiavelli and follow-up questions enhance student interest in the discussion. Finally, each chapter concludes with a useful reference list. The sixteen cases are designed to address issues as diverse as teacher incompetence, alcohol abuse, and censorship of poems — right out of the newspapers in thousands of towns across our country.

REFLECTIONS ON THE RESEARCH BASE OF THE TEXT

As stated in the preface, the skills are derived from extensive readings and an experimental study conducted in California involving the opinions of school superintendents and principals. In this way, we have tried to inform the practical application of the case studies with well-grounded academic research. Many different taxonomies of skills are available, but all seem to advance the theory that all skills are important in such a complex job as the principalship. One cannot advance his or her career without well-developed human, conceptual, technical, and socialization skills. In addition, there is not much time to acquire these skills on the job. How swiftly a beginning principal masters these skills will determine his or her ultimate success.

MOST IMPORTANT SKILLS MAY BE HARDEST TO MASTER

Most students appear to be fairly skilled in picking up the technical side of school administration. They can apply the education code. They are able to develop an equipment inventory and create a computerized class-registration system. With practice, they are able to develop a school budget.

But many students feel that the most important skill — creating a vision and motivating a group of teachers to follow that vision — is very difficult to do. They also find that they need to develop skills in communication, channeling conflict, and facilitating groups of all sizes. These skills are difficult to teach and are best learned through case study and actual experience. There is no doubt that on-the-job experience does fill in some of the gaps in the student's professional repertoire.

Finally, this text fills an important function as it melds theory and practice, encourages an intense discussion of both, and presents the opportunity to debate on a series of challenging and intriguing case studies.

DR. JUNE SCHMIEDER
Pepperdine University

DR. DONALD CAIRNS
Montana State University

Acheson, K. and Gall, M. (1992). *Techniques in the clinical supervision of teachers: Preservice and inservice applications.* White Plains, NY: Longman Publishing Co.

Airasian, P. W. (1985). *The ninth mental measurements yearbook, Volume I.* Buros Institute of Mental Measurements, University of Nebraska, Lincoln, NE. Iowa Tests of Basic Skills, Forms 7 and 8, Boston College, Chestnut Hill, MA.

Alexander, K. and Alexander, D. (1992). *American Public School Law.* Third edition. St. Paul, MN: West Publishing Co.

Arons, S. (1981). The crusade to ban books. *Education Digest,* 47(3):2−5.

Astuto, T. A. (1985). Meta-analysis of case studies of instructionally effective schools. *Urban Education,* 19(4):331−356.

Austin, G. R. (1979). Exemplary schools and the search for effectiveness. *Educational Leadership,* 37(1):10−14.

Averch, H. A., Carroll, S. J., Donaldson, T. S., Kiesling, H. J. and Pincus, J. (1972). *How effective is schooling? A critical review and synthesis of research findings.* Englewood Cliffs, NJ: Educational Technology Publications, pp. 166−182.

Azumi, J. and Madhere, S. (1982). *Characteristics of high achieving elementary schools.* Newark, NJ: Office of Research, Evaluations and Testing. Newark Board of Education (ERIC Document Reproduction Service No. ED 217 099).

Bacharach, S. B. and Lawler, E. J. (1980). *Power and politics in organizations.* San Francisco, CA: Jossey-Bass Inc.

Bacharach, S. B. and Mitchell S. M. (1983a). *The generation of practical theory: Schools as political institutions.* Ithaca, NY: State University of New York, School of Industrial and Labor Relations at Cornell University (ERIC Document Reproduction Service No. ED 243 176).

Bacharach, S. B. and Mitchell, S. M. (1983b). *Notes on a political theory of educational organizations. Consensus and power in school organizations.* Ithaca, NY: State University of New York, School of Industrial and Labor Relations (ERIC Document Reproduction Service No. ED 243 175).

Bailey, F. G. (1965). Decisions by consensus in councils and committees: With specific reference to village and local government of India. In M. Banton (ed.). *Political system and the distribution of power.* Columbus, OH: Frederich A. Prager Publishers, pp. 1−20.

Baker, L. E., Carrol, M., Clark, D., Lotto, L. and McKibbin, S. (1981). *Alternative perspectives for viewing educational organizations.* San Francisco, CA: Far West Regional Laboratories (ERIC Document Reproduction Service No. ED 206-088).

Baldridge, J. V. and Deal, T. E. (eds.). (1975). *Managing change in educational organizations: Sociological perspectives, strategies and case studies.* Berkeley, CA: McCutchan.

Barge, K. (1994). *Leadership: Communication skills for organizations and groups.* New York, NY: St. Martin's Press.

Barnard, C. (1948). *The functions of the executive.* Cambridge, MA: Harvard University Press.

Barrett, S. Unpublished film slides. Springfield School District No. 19. 525 Mill Street, Springfield, OR 97477.

Becker, H.S. (1961). The teacher in the authority system of complex organizations. In A. Etzioni (ed.). *Complex organizations: A sociological reader.* New York, NY: Holt, Rhinehart, and Winston, p. 30.

Behling, H. E., Jr. (1984). The effective school. *Monograph series, 10.* Baltimore, MD: Maryland Association of Teacher Educators, Maryland State Department of Education (ERIC Document Reproduction Service No. ED 257 222).

Berger, M. (1981). Coping with anarchy in organizations. In Pfeiffer, J. (ed.). *The 1981 annual handbook for group facilitators.* San Diego, CA: University Associates.

Berne, E. (1964). *Games people play.* New York, NY: Grove Press.

Bidwell, C. (1965). The school as a formal organization. In March, J. (ed.). *The handbook of organizations.* 1965. Chicago, IL: Rand McNally Publishers.

Black, J. and English, F. (1986). *What they don't tell you in schools of education about school administration.* Lancaster, PA: Technomic Publishing Co., Inc., pp. 53–62.

Blase, J. J. (1987). Dimensions of effective school leadership: The teacher's perspective. *American Research Journal,* 24(4):589–610.

Blumberg, A. (1984). The craft of school administration and some other rambling thoughts. *Educational Administration Quarterly,* 20(4):24–40.

Bondesio, M. (August 1992). Conflict management at school: An unavoidable task. Paper presented at the meeting of the Society for Regional Conference of the Commonwealth Council for Education Administration, Hong Kong.

Bonnie, P. T. (1994). *Federal disability law, American disabilities act.* West Nutshell Series, St. Paul, MN: West Publishing Co.

Bonstingel, J. (1992). *Schools of quality: An introduction to total quality management in education.* Alexandria, VA: Association for Supervision and Curriculum Development.

Bossert, S., Dwyer, D., Rowan, B. and Lee, G. (1982). The instructional management role of the principal. *Educational Administration Quarterly,* 18(3):34–64.

Bowers, D. and Seashore, S. (1966). Predicting organizational effectiveness with a four factor theory or leadership. *Administrative Science Quarterly,* 311:238–263.

Boyd, W. and Crowson, R. (1981). The changing conception and practice of public school administration. *Review of Research in Education,* 9:311–373.

Braden, W. W. (1988). *Abraham Lincoln: Public speaker.* Baton Rouge, LA: University Press.

Brookhover, W. B. (1981). Effective secondary schools. Philadelphia, PA: Research for Better Schools (ERIC Document Reproductions Service No. ED 231 088).

Brookhover, W. B. (1987). Distortion and overgeneralization are no substitute for sound research. *Phi Delta Kappan,* 69(3):225–227.

Brookhover, W., Beady, C., Flood, P., Schweitzer, J. and Wisenbaker, J. (1977). Schools can make a difference. East Lansing, MI: College of Urban Development, Michigan State University (ERIC Documentation Reproduction Service No. ED 145 034).

Brookhover, W., Gigliotti, R. J., Henderson, R. D., and Schneider, J. M. (1973). Elementary school social environment and school achievement. Final Report. East Lansing, MI: College of Urban Development, Michigan State University (ERIC Document Reproduction Service No. ED 086 306).

Brookhover, W. B. and Lezotte, L. W. (1979). Changes in school characteristics coincident with changes in student achievement. East Lansing, MI: Institute for Research on Teaching (252 Erickson Hall, 48824), Michigan State University. Occasional Paper No. 17.

Brouge, G. E. (1985). *The enemies of leadership: Lessons for leaders in education.* Bloomington, IN: Phi Delta Kappa.

Brundage, D. (ed.). (1979). *The journalism research fellows report: What makes an effective school?* Washington, D.C.: George Washington University.

Burns, J. M. (1978). *Leadership.* New York, NY: Harper Row, Inc.

Bureau of School Programs Evaluation, New York State Department of Education: Albany, New York. (1976). *Three strategies for studying the effects of school processes: An expanded edition of what factors relate to learning?* University of the State of New York (ERIC Document Reproduction Service No. ED 126 572).

Burlingame, M. (1980). Protecting private realities by managing public symbols: Mystifications, cover-ups, and martyrdom. Paper presented at the annual meeting of the American Educational Research Association, Boston, MA (ERIC Document Reproduction Service No. ED 191 164).

Burrup, P., Brimely, V. and Garfield, R. (1993). *Financing education in a climate of change.* Needham Heights, MA: Simon and Schuster.

Cairns, D. (1990). Differences in organizational structure between selected rural elementary and secondary schools in Washington State. Unpublished doctoral dissertation, Washington State University, Pullman, Washington.

Calonius, E. (1991). The big payoff from lotteries. *Fortune,* March 25:109.

Caliguri, J., Krueger, J. P. and Bailey, E. R. (1984). *Bureaucratic versus loose coupling governance: Ownership or chaos in managing conflict?* University of Missouri at Kansas City, MO (ERIC Document Reproduction Service No. ED 253 920).

Campbell, R., Cunningham, L., McPhee, R. and Nystrad, R. (1970). *The organization and control of American schools.* Fourth edition. Columbus, OH: Charles E. Merrill Publishing Company.

Caplan, M. K. and O'Rourke, T. J. (1988). Improving student achievement on standardized tests: One approach. *NASSP Bulletin,* 72(505):54−58.

Cetron, M. J. and Gayle, M. E. (1990). Educational renaissance: 43 trends for U.S. schools. *The Futurist,* pp. 34−37.

Charters, W. W. Jr. (1975). Role coupling in the schools work system: Operationalizing task interdependence among teaching personnel. Working paper prepared for a meeting of the task group on educational systems as loosely coupled organization. LaJolla, CA (ERIC Document Reproduction Service No. ED 283 291).

Clark, D., Lotto, L. and Astuto, T. (1984). Effective schools and school improvement: A comparative analysis of two lines of inquiry. *Educational Administration Quarterly,* 20(3):41−68.

Clark, D., Lotto, L. and McCarthy, M. (1980). Factors associated with success in urban elementary schools. *Phi Delta Kappan*, 61(7):467−470.

Clark, D. L. and McKibbin, S. (1982). From orthodoxy to pluralism: New views of school administration. *Phi Delta Kappan*, 63(10):669−672.

Clark, T. A. and McCarthy, D. P. (1983). School improvement in New York City: The evolution of a project. *Educational Researcher*, 12(4):17−23.

Cohen, M. D. and March, J. G. (1974). *Leadership and ambiguity. Report for the Carnegie Commission on higher education.* New York, NY: McGraw-Hill Book Company.

Cohen, M. D., March, J. G. and Olson, J. P. (1972). A garbage can model of organizational choice. *Administrative Science Quarterly*, 17(1):1−25.

Coleman, J. S., Campbell, E., Hobson, C., McPartland, J., Mood, A., Weinfeld, F. and York, R. (1966). *Equality of Educational Opportunity.* Washington, D.C.: U.S. Department of Education, National Center for Education Statistics.

Cooperman, S. and Bloom, J. (1985). *Getting the most from the New Jersey HSPT: A practical guide to resolving curriculum design and delivery problems.* Farmington, MA: Center for Teaching and Learning Mathematics (ERIC Document Reproduction Service No. ED 278 713).

Corbett, D. H. (1991). Community influence and school micropolitics. In Blase, J. (ed.). *The politics of life in schools: Power, conflict and cooperation.* Newbury Park, CT: Sage Publications.

Corwin, R. G. (1974). The formulation of goals in the public schools. In Hasenfeld, Y. and English, R. (eds.). *Human service organizations: A book of readings.* Ann Arbor, MI: University of Michigan Press.

Crowell, R. (1986). *Curriculum alignment.* Washington, D.C.: Office of Research and Improvement (ERIC Document Reproduction Service No. ED 280 874).

Crowson, R. and Morris, V. C. (1982). The principal's role in organizational goal attainment: Discretionary management at the school site level. Paper presented at the annual meeting of the American Educational Research Association, New York (ERIC Document Reproduction Service No. ED 218 766).

Crowson, R. L. and Porte-Gerhie, C. (1980). The discretionary behavior of principals. *Educational Administrative Quarterly*, 16(1):45−69.

Curriculum Alignment with the Essential Learning Skills. (1985). Unpublished materials, Oregon State Department of Education, 700 Pringle Parkway SE, Salem, OR 97310-0290.

Cusick, P. A. (1981). A study of networks among professional staffs in secondary schools. *Educational Administrative Quarterly*, 17(3):114−138.

Daresh, J. and Playko, M. (1989). In search of critical skills for beginning principals. Paper presented at the annual meeting of the University Council for Educational Administration, Phoenix, AR.

Data Research Inc. (1994). *Desktop encyclopedia of American school law.* Rosemont, MN: Author.

Deal, T. E. (1985). The symbolism of effective schools. *The Elementary School Journal*, 85(5):601−620.

Deal, T. E. and Celotti, L. D. (1980). How much influence do (can) educational administrators have on classrooms? *Phi Delta Kappan*, 61(7):471−473.

Deal, T. and Kennedy, A. (1982). *Corporate cultures.* Reading, MA: Addison-Wesley.

Digest of Education Statistics. (1988). National Center for Education Statistics. U.S. Department of Education. Office of Educational Research and Improvement. U.S. Government Printing Office; Superintendent of Documents, Washington, D.C.

Doherty, V. and Peters, L. (1981). Goals and objectives in educational planning and evaluation. *Educational Leadership,* 38:606−611.

Donelson, K. (1987). Six statements/questions from the censors. *Phi Delta Kappan,* 69(3):208−214.

Dornbush, S. M. and Scott, W. R. (1975). *Evaluation and the exercise of authority: A theory of control applied to diverse organizations.* San Francisco, CA: Jossey-Bass.

Duckett, W., Park, D., Clark, D., McCarthy, M., Lotto, L., Gregory, L, Herilhy, J. and Burelson, D. L. (1980). *Why do some schools succeed? The Phi Delta Kappan study of exceptional urban elementary schools.* Bloomington, IN: Phi Delta Kappa (ERIC Document Reproduction Service No. ED 194 660).

Earnest, G. et al. (1993). Styles as reflections of Jungian personality type preferences of cooperative extension's north central region directors and district directors. Research report No. SR 71. Columbus, OH: Ohio State University, Department of Agricultural Education.

Edmonds, R. R. (1979a). *A discussion of the literature and issues related to effective schooling* (ERIC Document Reproduction Service No. ED 170 394).

Edmonds. R. (1979b). Effective schools for the urban poor. *Educational Leadership,* 37(1):15−24.

Edmonds, R. R. (1983). *An overview of school improvement programs.* Washington, D.C.: Report to National Institute of Education (ERIC Document Reproduction Service No. ED 250 790).

Edmonds, R. R. and Frederiksen, J. R. (1979). *Search for effective schools: The identification and analysis of city schools that are instructionally effective for poor children* (ERIC Document Reproduction Service No. 170 396).

English, F. (1987). *Curriculum management for schools, colleges, and business.* Springfield, IL: Charles C. Thomas Publishing.

Erickson, D. A. (1979). Research on educational administration: The state of the art. *Educational Researcher,* 8(3):9−14.

Equal Employment Opportunity Commission, Title VII of the Civil Rights Act of 1964.

Evans, C. (1988). In defense of *Huckleberry Finn:* Antiracism motifs in *Huckleberry Finn* and a review of racial criticism in Twain's work. Unpublished doctoral dissertation, Rice University.

Fairman, M. and Clark, E. (1985). Moving towards excellence: A model to increase student productivity. *NASSP Bulletin,* 69(477):6−11.

Featherstone, R. L. and Hickey, H. W. (1985). Situational planning: The politicians delight. *School Administrator,* 42(1):16−17.

Fedler, P. (1991). Schoolbook selection and reconsidered policies for managing challenges to schoolbook in Nebraska. Unpublished doctoral dissertation, University of Nebraska.

Felsenthal, H. (1982). Factors influencing school effectiveness: An ecological analysis of an effective school. Paper resented at the annual meeting of the American Research Association, New York, NY (ERIC Document Reproduction Service No. ED 214 299).

Fetters, W., Collins, E. F. and Smith, J. W. (1968). *Characteristics differentiating under and over-achieving elementary schools.* Washington D.C.: National Center for Educational Statistics (DHEW) Division of Data Analysis and Dissemination (ERIC Document Reproduction Service No. ED 021 318).

Firestone, W. A. and Herriott, R. E. (1982b). Prescriptions for effective elementary schools don't fit secondary schools. *Educational Leadership*, 40(3):51–53.

Firestone, W. A. and Herriott, R. E. (1982a). *Rational bureaucracy or loosely coupled system?* Philadelphia, PA: Research for Better Schools (ERIC Document Reproduction Service No. ED 238 096).

Firestone, W. A. and Wilson, B. L. (1984). What can principals do? Culture is a key to more effective instruction. *NASSP Bulletin*, 68:7–11.

Firestone, W. A. and Herriott, R. E., (1981). The bureaucratic elementary school: Comparing two images of elementary, jr. high and high schools. Paper presented at the annual meeting of the American Educational Research Association, Los Angeles, CA (ERIC Document Reproduction Service No. ED 203 532).

Fischer, L., Schimmel, D. and Kelly, C. (1994). *Teachers and the law.* Fourth edition. White Plains, NY: Longman Publishing Inc.

Fisher, W. and Koue, G. (1991). Conflict management. *Library Administration and Management*, 5(3):145–146, 148–150.

Fortune, J. C. and Cromack, T. R. (1987). *Test critiques, Volume III.* Test Corporation of America. Metropolitan Achievement Test: 5th Edition. Blacksburg, VA: Polytechnic Institute and State University.

Foster, W. (1983). *Loose coupling revisited: A critical view of Weick's contribution to educational administration.* Victoria, Australia, Deakin University Press (ERIC Document Reproduction Service No. ED 283 255).

Fry, E. (1980). Test review: Metropolitan achievement tests. *The reading teacher.* New Brunswick, NJ: Rutgers University.

Gay, L. R. (1987). *Educational research: Competencies for analysis and application.* Columbus, OH: Merrill Publishing Company.

Gemelch, W. and Carroll, J. (1991). The three Rs of conflict management for department chairs and faculty. *Innovative Higher Education*, 18(3):107–123.

Getzels, J. W. (1958). Administration as a social process. In Halprin, A. (ed.). *Administrative Theory in Education.* Chicago, IL: Midwest Administrative Center, pp. 140–165.

Gigliotti, R. J. and Brookhover, W. (1975). The learning environment: A comparison of high and low achieving elementary schools. *Urban Education*, 20(3):245–261.

Glasser, W. (1994). *The control theory manager.* New York, NY: Harper Collins Publishers, Inc.

Goodlad, J. I. (1984). *A place called school.* New York, NY: McGraw-Hill Book Co.

Gross, N. and Herriott, R.E. (1965). *Staff leadership in public schools: A sociological inquiry.* New York, NY: John Wiley.

Gutek, G. L. (1984–85). *Standard education almanac.* Seventeenth edition. Chicago, IL: Professional Publications.

Hage, J. and Akien, M. (1974). Routine technology, social structure, and organizational goals. In Hasenfeld, Y. and English, R. (eds.). *Human service organizations: A book of readings.* Ann Arbor, MI: University of Michigan Press.

Hall, G. and Hord, S. (1987). *Change in schools: Facilitating the process.* Albany, NY: State University of New York Press.

Hall, R. (1963). The concept of bureaucracy. *American Journal of Sociology,* 69:32−40.

Halprin, A. (1967). *Theory and research in administration.* New York, NY: MacMillan Publishing.

Hannaway, J. and Sproul, L.S. (1978−79). Who's running the show? Coordination and control in educational organizations. *Administrator's Notebook,* 27(9):1−4.

Hanson, M. E. (1985). *Educational administration and organizational behavior.* Second edition. Boston, MA: Allyn & Bacon Publishing, pp. 5-49.

Hanson, M. (1991). *Educational administration and organizational behavior.* Third edition. Needham Heights, MA: Allyn & Bacon Publishing, pp. 142−148.

Hartley, M. (1985). Leadership style and conflict resolution: No man(ager) is an island. *Journal of Cooperative Education,* 21(2):16−23.

Hathaway, W. et al. (1985). *A regional and local item response theory based on a test item bank system.* Portland Public Schools, Department of Research and Evaluation (ERIC Document Reproduction Service No. ED 284 883).

Hechinger, P. (1988). Does school structure matter? *Educational Researcher,* 17(6):10−13.

Henson, K. T. and Saterfiel, T. H. (1985). State mandated accountability programs: Are they educationally sound? *NASSP Bulletin,* 69(477):23−27.

Herriott, R. E. and Hodgkins, B. J. (1974). Social context and the school: An open system analysis of social and educational change. In Hasenfeld, Y. and English, R. (eds.). *Human service organizations: A book of readings.* Ann Arbor, MI: University of Michigan Press.

Herriott, R. E. and Firestone, W. A. (1984). Two images of schools as organizations: A refinement and elaboration. *Educational Administration Quarterly,* 20(4):41−57.

Hersey, P. and Blanchard, K. (1977). *Management of organizational behavior: Utilizing human resources.* Second edition. Englewood Cliffs, NJ: Prentice-Hall.

Hersey, P. and Blanchard, K. (1982). *Management of organizational behavior: Utilizing human resources.* Third edition. Englewood Cliffs, NJ: Prentice-Hall.

Hersey, P. and Blanchard, K. (1988). *Management of organizational behavior: Utilizing human resources.* Fifth edition. Englewood Cliffs, NJ: Prentice-Hall.

Hersey, P. and Blanchard, K. (1993). *Management of organizational behavior: Utilizing human resources.* Sixth edition. Englewood Cliffs, NJ: Prentice-Hall.

Hertel, E. H. (1985). *Metropolitan Achievement Tests.* Fifth Edition. *The ninth mental measurements yearbook.* In J. V. Mitchell, Jr. (ed.). Buros Institute of Mental Measurements, University of Nebraska-Lincoln. Lincoln, NE: University of Nebraska Press.

Heslep, R. (1988). *Professional ethics and the Georgia Public School Administrator.* Athens, GA: University of Georgia, Bureau of Educational Services.

Hosman, C. (1990). Superintendent selection and dismissal: A changing community defines its values. *Urban Education,* 25(3):350−369.

Hoy, W. K. and Ferguson, J. (1985). A theoretical framework and exploration of organizational effectiveness of schools. *Educational Administration Quarterly,* 31(2):117−134.

Iannaconne, L. and Lutz, F. (1970). *Politics, power and policy: The governing of local school districts.* Columbus, OH: Charles E. Merrill.

Irvine, D. L. (1979). Factors associated with school effectiveness. *Educational Technology,* 29(5): 53−55.

Isherwood, E. (1973). The principal and his authority: An empirical study. *The High School Journal,* 56(6):291−303.

Jencks, C. and Bartlett, S. (1972). *Who gets ahead: The determinants of economic success in America.* New York, NY: Basic Books.

Johnson, C. L. (1994). *Stifled laughter: One woman's story about fighting censorship.* Golden, CO: Fulcrum Publishing.

Johnston, J. H. (1987). Values, culture and the effective schools. *NAASP Bulletin,* 71(497):79−88.

Kanter, R. M. (1989). *When giants learn to dance: Mastering the challenge of strategy, management, and careers in the 1990s.* New York: Simon and Schuster.

Kanter, R. M. (1989). *The changemasters: Innovations for productivity in the American corporation.* New York: Simon and Schuster.

Kaplan, R. E. (1982). Intervention in a loosely organized system: An encounter with non-being. *Journal of Applied Behavior Sciences,* 18(3):415−432.

Kelly, T. F. (1988). *Practical Strategies for School Improvement.* Unpublished Manuscript.

Kelly, T. F. and Rooney, S. M. (1989). New York State education department effective schools consortium survey: Reliability and validity. *The Effective School Report,* 1(3):3−4.

Kerr, N. (1964). The school board as an agency of legitimation. *Sociology of Education,* 38:34−59.

Kirkendall, R. (1966). Discriminating social, economic, and political characteristics of changing versus stable policy making systems in school districts. Unpublished doctoral dissertation, Claremont Graduate School.

Kirst, M. (1981). Loss of support for public secondary schools: Some causes and solutions. *Daedalus,* 110:45−68.

La Morte, M. (1992). *School law: Cases and concepts.* Boston, MA: Allyn & Bacon Publishing.

Lezotte, L. W. (1984). *School effectiveness research: A tribute to Ron Edmonds. One perspective on an effective schools research agenda.* Paper presented at the annual meeting of the American Educational Research Association, New Orleans (ERIC Document Reproduction Service No. ED 253 961).

Lezotte, L. W. and Bancroft, B. A. (1986). School improvement based upon effective schools research. *Outcomes, a Quarterly Journal of the Network for Outcome Based Schools,* 6(1):13−17.

Liberman, A. and Miller, L. (eds.). (1984). *Teachers, their world, and their work: Implications for school.* Alexandria, VA: Association for Supervision and Curriculum Development.

Lortie, D. (1969). The Balance of Control and Autonomy in Elementary School Teaching. In A. Etzioni (ed.). *The semi professions and their organization.* New York, NY: Free Press, pp. 1−53.

Lortie, D. (1975). *School teacher.* Chicago, IL: University of Chicago Press, chapter 8.

Lotto, L. S. (1984). Solutions in search of problems: The experiential validity of new view on educational administration. Paper presented at the annual meeting of the American Educational Research Association, New Orleans (ERIC Document Reproduction Service No. ED 245 408).

Lutz, F. and Iannaconne, L. (1978). *Public participation in local school districts.* Lexington, MA: D. C. Heath and Company.

Lyman, L. (1988). The principal: Responsive leadership in times of change. Paper presented at the annual meeting of United School Administrators of Kansas. Wichita, KS (ERIC Document Reproduction Services No. ED 293 201).

MacKenzie, D. (1983). Research for school improvement: An appraisal of some recent trends. *Educational Researcher,* 12(4):5−14.

MacPhail-Wilcox, B. and Guth, J. (1983). Effectiveness research and school administration: Both sides of the coin. *NASSP Bulletin,* 67(465):3−8.

Macy, K. P. (1986). An empirical study of the organizational structure and co-ordination of large and small, public and non-public high schools in Minnesota−Some considerations for educational leaders. *Dissertation Abstracts International,* 47 AAC #862 7028.

Mann, D. (1986). Testimony given in support of H. B. 747. *Outcomes,* 6(1):10.

Mann, D. and Inman, D. (1984). Improving education within existing resources: The instructionally effective schools approach. *Journal of Educational Finance,* 10(2):256−269.

March, J. E. and Olson, J. P. (1976). *Ambiguity and choice in organizations.* Bergen, Norway: Universitetsforlagets.

March, J. (1978). American public school administration: A short analysis. *School Review,* 86(2):217−219.

Maryland State Department of Education. (1978). *Process evaluation: A comprehensive study of outliers.* Baltimore: The Maryland State Department of Education (ERIC Document Reproduction Service No. ED 160 644).

Mayo, E. (1945). *The social problems of an industrial civilization.* Boston, MA: Division of Research, Graduate School of Business Administration, Harvard University.

McGuire, J. (1984). Strategies of school district conflict. *Sociology of Education,* 57(1):31−42.

Mehrens, W. A. (1984). National tests and local curriculum: Match or mismatch? *Educational Measurement: Issues and Practices,* Fall:9−15.

Meyer, J. W. and Scott, W. R. (1983). *Organizational environment ritual and rationality.* Beverly Hills, CA: Sage Publications.

Meyer, J. W., and Rowan, B. (1983). Institutionalized organizations: Formal structure as myth and ceremony. In Meyer, J. W. and Scot, R. S. (eds.). *Organizational environments: Ritual and rationality.* Beverly Hills, CA: Sage Publications.

Miller, S. L., Cohen, S. R. and Sayre, K. A. (1985). Significant achievement gains using the effective school model. *Educational Leadership,* March:38−43.

Mintsberg, N. (1973). *The nature of managerial work.* New York, NY: Harper and Row.

Monroe, C. et al. (1989). Conflict behaviors of difficult subordinates. *Southern Communication Journal,* 54(4):311−329.

Moore, K. (1988). *Influences of censorship challenges on state textbook adoption criteria which affect school curriculum.* University of the Pacific.

Morrill, C. and Thomas, C. (1992). Organizational conflict management as disputing process: The problem of social escalation. *Human Communication Research,* 18(3):400−428.

Morris, V. C., Crowson, R. L., Hurwitz, E. and Porter-Gerhie, C. (1981). *The urban principal: Discretionary decision making in a large educational organization.* Washington D.C.: National Institute of Education (# NIE-G-79-0019) (ERIC Document Reproduction Service No. ED 207 178).

Murphy, J. and Hallinger, P. (1985). Effective high schools−What are the common characteristics? *NASSP Bulletin,* 69(477):18−22.

Murphy, J. A., Hallinger, P. and Mesa, R. P. (1984). Strategies for coupling schools: The effective schools approach. *Educational Evaluation and Policy Analysis,* 6(1):5−13.

Murphy, J., Weil, M., Hallinger, P. and Mitman, A. (1985). School effectiveness: A conceptional framework. *The Educational Forum,* 49(3):361−374.

New York City Board of Education. (1979). *School improvement project: The case study phase.* New York, NY: School Improvement Project.

National Center of Alcohol Education. (1982). *Planning alcoholism counseling education (PACE): A curriculum and instructional resource guide.* Arlington, VA: National Center for Alcohol Education.

Nidermeyer, F. and Yelon, S. (1981). Los Angeles aligns instruction with essential learning skills. *Educational Leadership,* May:618−620.

Oliver, A. O. (1993). The politics of textbook controversy: Parents' challenge of a reading series. Unpublished doctoral dissertation, University of Wisconsin.

Orlich, D. (1989). Staff development: Enhancing the human potential. Boston, MA: Allyn & Bacon Publishing.

Ouchi, W. G. (1978). Coupled versus uncoupled control in organizational hierarchies. In Myer, M. W. (ed.). *Environment and organizations.* San Francisco, CA: Jossey-Bass, pp. 264−289.

Ouchi, W. G. (1981). *Theory z.* Reading, MA: Addison-Wesley.

Ouchi, W. G. and Price, R. W. (1978). Hierarchies, clans and theory z: A new perspective on organizational development. *Organizational Dynamics,* 1(2):24−45.

Owens, R. G. (1985). American high school as a clan: Dynamics of organization and leadership. Paper presented at the annual meeting of American Educational Research Association. Chicago, IL (ERIC Document Reproduction Service No. ED 262 480).

Owens, R. G. (1995). *Organizational behavior in education.* Fifth edition. Needham Heights, MA: Allyn & Bacon, pp. 146−165.

Parkay, F., Currie, G. and Rhodes, J. (1992). Professional socialization: A longitudinal study of first time high school principals. *Educational Administrative Quarterly,* 28:43−75.

Perrow, C. (1974). The analysis of goals in complex organizations. In Hasenfeld, Y. and English, R. A. (eds.). *Human service organizations: A book of readings.* Ann Arbor, MI: The Univerity of Michigan Press.

Perrow, C. (1978). Demystifying organizations. In Sarri and Hasenfeld (eds.). *The management of human services.* New York, NY: Columbia University Press.

Peters, J. J. and Waterman, R. H., Jr. (1982). *In search of excellence: Lessons from America's best-run companies.* New York, NY: Harper and Row Publishers.

Peterson, P. E. (1976). *School politics Chicago style.* Chicago, IL: The University of Chicago Press.

Peterson, K., Murphy, J. and Hallinger, P. (1987). Superintendents' perception of the control and coordination of the technical core in effective school districts. *Educational Administration Quarterly,* 23(1):79−95.

Phillips, D. T. (1992). *Lincoln on leadership.* New York, NY: Time Warner Books.

Purkey, S. C. and Smith, M. S. (1983). Effective schools−A review. *Elementary School Journal,* 83:427−452.

Rada, R. (1984). Community dissatisfaction and school governance. *Planning and Changing,* 15(4):234−247.

Rada, R. (1989). A political context framework for the study of local school governance. Unpublished manuscript.

Richards, D. M. (1986). Productive and effective schools. Paper presented at the annual meeting of the American Educational Finance Association, Chicago, IL (ERIC Document Reproduction Service No. ED 268 637).

Roberts, W. (1987). *Leadership secrets of Attila the Hun.* New York, NY: Warner Books.

Rothstein, L. (1995). *Special education law.* Second edition. White Plains, NY: Longman Publishing Inc.

Rowan B., Bossert, S. and Dwyer, D. (1983). Research on effective schools: A cautionary note. *Educational Researcher,* 12(4):24−31.

Rutter, M., Maughum, B., Mortimore, P., Ouston, J. and Smith, A. (1979). *Fifteen thousand hours: Secondary schools and their effects on children.* Cambridge, MA: Harvard University Press.

California school effectiveness study, The first year (1974−75). Sacramento, CA: Office of Program Evaluation and Research; California State Department of Education.

Salganik, L. H. (1985). Schools under pressure: The external environment and recent organizational reforms. Chicago. Paper presented at the annual meeting of the American Educational Association (ERIC Document Reproduction Service No. ED 265 636).

Sarason, B. (1971). *The culture of the school and the problem of change.* Boston, MA: Allyn & Bacon Publishing.

Schmieder, J. H. and Townley, A. J. (1994). *School finance: A California perspective.* Dubuque, IA: Kendall Hunt Publishing.

Schmieder, J. H., McGrevin, C. Z. and Townley, A. J. (1984). Keys to success: Critical skills for novice principals. *Journal of School Leadership,* 4(3):272−293.

Scott, W. R. (1981). *Organizations: Rational, natural and open systems.* Englewood Cliffs, NJ: Prentice-Hall.

Sharpe, D. (1984). *Choosing leadership styles.* Montana State University Extension Service Bulletin No. MT 8404.

Shiro, Dora. (1985). *Safe schools, sound schools: Learning in a non-disruptive environment.* New York, NY: Teachers College Press, Columbia University (ERIC Document Reproduction Service No. ED 253 602).

Shoop, R. J. (1992). *School law for the principal.* Needham Heights, MA: Allyn & Bacon Publishing.

Sizemore, B. A. (1985). Pitfalls and promises of effective schools research. *Journal of Negro Education,* 54(3):269−288.

Spady, G. W. and Marx, G. (1984). *Excellence in our schools: Making it happen.* Arlington, VA: American Association of School Administrators and Far West Laboratory.

Spartz, J. L., Valdes, A. L., McCormick, W. J., Myers, J. and Geppart, W. J. (1977). *Delaware educational accountability system case studies: Elementary grades 1 – 4.* Dover, DE: Delaware Department of Instruction (Report of Results).

Sproull, L., Weiner, S. and Wolf, D. (1978). *Organizing an anarchy: Belief, bureaucracy and politics in the National Institute of Education.* Chicago, IL: The University of Chicago Press.

Squires, D. (1980). *Characteristics of effective schools: The importance of school processes.* Philadelphia, PA: Research for Better Schools, Inc. (ERIC Document Reproduction Service No. 197 486).

Stallings, J. A. and Mohlman, G. (1981). *School policy, leadership style, teacher change and student behavior in eight secondary schools.* Mountain View, CA. Prepared for the National Institute of Education Stallings Teaching and Learning Institute.

Stedman, L. C. (1985). A new look at the effective school literature. *Urban Education,* 29(3):295 – 326.

Stedman, L. C. (1987). It's time we changed the effective schools formula. *Phi Delta Kappan,* 69(3):215 – 223.

Stevens, B. (1985). *School effectiveness: Eight variables that make a difference.* Lansing MI: Michigan State Board of Education (ERIC Document Reproduction Service No. ED 217 218).

Tagiari, R. (1968). The concept of organizational climate. In Tagiari and G.H. Litwen (eds.). *Organizational climate: Exploration of a concept.* Boston, MA: Harvard University, Division of Research, Graduate School of Business Administration.

Thomas, G., Sperry, D. and Wasden, F. (1991). *The law and teacher employment.* St. Paul, MN: West Publishing Co., pp. 103 – 107.

Thompson, J. D. (1967). *Organizations in action.* New York, NY: McGraw-Hill Book Co.

Tucker, B. (1994). *Federal disability law.* Nutshell series. Saint Paul, MN: West Publishing Co.

Valente, W. D. (1994). *Law in the Schools.* Third edition. New York, NY: Merrill Publishing Co., pp. 238 – 239.

Vidich, A. and Bensman, J. (1968). *Small town in mass society: class, power, and religion in a rural community.* Princeton, NJ: Princeton University Press.

Walton, M. (1986). *The Deming management method.* New York, NY: Perigree Books.

Webb, D. et al. (1987). *Personnel administration in education.* Columbus, OH: Merrill Publishing Company, pp. 77 – 91.

Weber, G. (1971). *Inner-city children can be taught to read: Four successful schools.* Washington, D.C.: CBE Occasional Papers No. 18, Council for Basic Education.

Weber, M. (1947). The theory of social and economic organizations. Henderson and Parsons, (eds.). New York, NY: MacMillan.

Weick, K. E. (1976). Educational organizations as loosely coupled systems. *Administrative Science Quarterly,* 21:1 – 19.

Weick, K. (1979). *The Social Psychology of Organizing.* Second edition. Reading, MA: Addison-Wesley Publishing Company.

Weick, K. E. (1982). Administering education in loosely coupled systems. *Phi Delta Kappan,* 63(10):673–676.

Wellisch, J. B., MacQueen, A. H., Carrier, R. and Duck, G. (1978). School management and organization in successful schools. *Sociology of Education,* 51(3):211–226.

Wheeless, L. and Reichel, L. (1990). A reinforcement model of the relationship of supervisors' general communication styles and conflict management styles to task attraction. *Communication Quarterly,* 38(4):372–387.

Whitford, B. L. and Kyle, D. W. (1984). Interdisciplinary teaming: Initiating change in a middle school. Paper presented at the annual meeting of the Educational Research Association, New Orleans (ERIC Document Reproduction Service No. ED 263 672).

Willower, D. J. and Smith, J. P. (1987). Organizational culture in schools: Myth and creation. *High School Journal,* 70:87–94.

Wilson, B. L. and Corbett, H. D. (1983). Organization and change: The effects of school linkages in quality of implementation. *Educational Administration Quarterly,* 19(4):85–104.

Wirt, F. and Kirst, W. (1972). *The political web of American schools.* Boston, MA: Little, Brown and Co.

Wirt, F. and Kirst, M. (1982). *The politics of education: Schools in conflict.* Berkeley, CA: McCutchan Publishing Corporation.

Zeigler, H., Jennings, M. and Peak, W. (1974). *Governing American schools: Political interaction in local school districts.* North Sciuate, MA: Duxbury Press.

Zuelke, D. and Willerman, M. (1992). *Conflict and decision making in elementary schools.* Dubuque, IA: Wm. C. Brown Publishing Inc.

Date Due

APR - 0 1997		
APR - 9 1997		
FEB 2 8 1998		
JUL - 7 2000		
DEC 1 0 2000		
JAN 20 R		
Feb 27 R		
APR 1 1 2001		
NOV 1 9 2001		
JAN 0 2 2001		